ANITA COBBY

THE CRIME THAT SHOCKED THE NATION

ANITA COBBY

THE CRIME THAT SHOCKED THE NATION

Alan J. Whiticker

First published in 2015 by New Holland Publishers
Sydney

Level 1, 178 Fox Valley Road, Wahroonga, NSW 2076, Australia

newhollandpublishers.com

A record of this book is held at the National Library of Australia.

ISBN 9781760796518

Managing Director: Fiona Schultz
Project Editor: Laura Fulton
Designer: Andrew Davies
Production Director: Arlene Gippert
Printed in China

10 9 8 7 6 5 4 3 2 1

Keep up with New Holland Publishers:

NewHollandPublishers
@newhollandpublishers

For the men and women who worked on the original Anita Cobby investigation in 1986.

Contents

Introduction

The abduction, pack-rape and murder of Anita Cobby in February 1986 has been described as one of Australia's most shocking crimes. Almost three decades after the body of the 26-year-old nurse was found in a paddock in Western Sydney, the appalling details of the young woman's final hours continue to resonate around the country. The subsequent capture and trial of the five men responsible for Anita's death generated both fear and loathing within the local community and led to calls for the return of the death penalty.

When I think back to the start of 1986, it's the stifling heat I remember most. I was a young schoolteacher at the time and my wife was heavily pregnant, expecting our first child. The January nights leading up to the start of the school year were very still, hot and humid, and I felt for my wife who had to battle through it with all the pains and discomfort associated with the final months of pregnancy ... without the luxury of air conditioning, I might add. It was, to coin a cliché, a long, hot summer.

Having gained a scholarship at Nepean Teacher's College in Kingswood in the late 1970s, I, like most of my friends, was teaching in the Western Suburbs, taking the first steps of promotion after surviving several years in what was widely regarded in educational circles as 'the wild, wild west.' I had recently moved schools from Blacktown to St Marys, having consciously tried to move closer to home now that my wife and I were starting our family.

I graduated from a Catholic school in Penrith, so it was only natural that I went into Catholic education when I graduated as a teacher. My first teaching appointment was at St Patrick's Primary School in Blacktown, opposite Westpoint Plaza and within walking distance of Blacktown Station. I was somewhat of a novelty there of sorts, the first male teacher employed by the Sisters of Mercy run school for more than a decade and, for a short while, the only male teacher on staff.

Among the many children I taught there, I particularly remember Linda McGaughey … not only because she was in one of the first classes I taught, but also because of later events that will become self-evident in this book. I also remember her older brother Paul, an athletic teenager who did a stint of work-experience on my class in the early 1980s. Like most of the other students from that area, they were great kids and came from a loving, working class family.

Sunday, 2 February 1986 was blistering hot. The previous night we had celebrated my father-in-law's 50th birthday, but Sunday was a quiet day leading up to the first full week of school. The world was still reeling in the aftermath of the Challenger Space Shuttle disaster the previous Tuesday, which claimed the lives of all seven astronauts 73 seconds into its flight. The tragedy was made all the more shocking because it was watched live on TV around the world. That one of the astronauts was a schoolteacher, Christa McAuliffe, who had been selected from literally of thousands of applicants, brought the tragedy a little closer to those of us who worked in education and who aspired for our students to reach for the stars.

The discovery of the body of a young woman, murdered and dumped in a paddock in Reen Road, Prospect, was just as shocking and very close to home. As the facts of the case unfolded, the community became both horrified and repulsed.

Newton Road – how many times had I driven down that road on my way home to Penrith? Every day of the school year, I imagine, for five years straight. Reen Road was known as a lover's lane at the bottom of a dirt road near Blacktown Drive-In. In those days, the M4 freeway ended at Prospect on the Great Western Highway, right next to the back of the boiler paddock where the body was found. Thinking of that desolated area, it was impossible not to be touched by the victim's fate.

But then, all of Australia was touched by the Anita Cobby case.

In writing this book, I don't claim to occupy any more special a place in the story other than that I was born, grew up, worked and raised my own family in Western Sydney. For me, the lives of Anita Cobby and the five men responsible for her death has always been more than an issue of 'good versus evil'. That would be an oversimplification of the impact the crime had on the people involved, the community and the law.

The purpose of this book, then, is to look at the impact of the Cobby case from as many different viewpoints as possible … the family, the detectives, the media and the law, to name just a few. Sadly, Anita's parents Garry and Grace Lynch are no longer with us. I was aware, however, that film producer Graham McNeice conducted one of the last major interviews with them for an episode of his Crime Investigation program in 2005, of which only a small portion was used. Graham generously allowed me to use the transcript of that extensive interview for this book.

Interviewing the former detectives who worked on the case was a real privilege. They were guarded at first but eventually opened up and talked about the investigation that lasted only several months but impacted greatly on the rest of their lives. Each of the detectives gave fascinating insights into what happened in Blacktown all those years ago. My sincere thanks to police chaplain Garry Raymond, a junior detective on the Cobby investigation who introduced me to some of the key men who investigated the original case – Ian 'Speed' Kennedy, who headed the task force, Garry Heskett, Graham Rosetta and Tony Waters – and also provided much-needed encouragement. I am also grateful to former detectives Tom Sharp and John Wakefield who provided vital background information.

The voices of others, including witness Paul McGaughey, news editor John Benaud and reporter Simon Bouda were also invaluable. Then there were the many journalists, authors and documentarians who covered the original case. Their words and testimonies are still powerful, 30 years later.

The tragedy remains, however, that Anita Cobby is no longer here to speak for herself. It would be easy as a writer to intellectualise and over-analyse what happened to the young nurse in Reen Road that summer's night, but having read many of the original transcripts of the case, viewed the crime scene photos and interviewed those people who were actually at the centre of the investigation, it's something I've been careful not to do.

Anita Cobby was a real person, and what happened to her was a tragedy.

Alan Whiticker, August 2015

Author's Note: Grace Lynch was known as 'Peg' by her family and friends. I never had the pleasure of meeting Mr and Mrs Lynch so I have opted to use her real name throughout this book, although other sources often refer to her by her nickname.

Of the five men gaoled for the murder of Anita Cobby, two were known as 'Mick' … Mick Murdoch and Mick Murphy. To avoid confusion, I have made reference to 'Michael Murdoch' and 'Mick Murphy' throughout this book.

Chapter One

The Times

She emerged out of the throng of people in Sydney's Martin Place like a ray of sunshine ... young, petite, neatly dressed, and with such a radiant, natural smile that the photographer taking black and white pictures of lunch-goers just had to snap it. As the young lady with the beauty queen looks climbed the stairs, she was beaming as she looked past the cameraman and fixed her sight on some far off destination. The girl was going places, and she had no time to stop and chat.
Her name was Anita Cobby.

The weekend newspapers on Sunday, 2 February 1986 were packed with coverage of the unsolved murder of Megan Kalajzich, wife of the owner of the Manly Pacific International Hotel on Sydney's Northern Beaches. Millionaire hotelier Andrew Kalajzich told police that in the early hours of 27 January, someone had broken into their Manly home and executed his wife with two shots from a .22 calibre rifle at close range. Mr Kalajzich had then jumped out of bed, narrowly avoiding two shots meant for him. Outside the Mary Immaculate Catholic Church on 1 February, 1500 mourners remembered Mrs Kalajzich as a 'warm, unassuming person' whose pre-mediated and planned execution was totally out of step with the rest of her life.

Police were also bewildered. How could a professional killer murder her with two shots from beside the bed and miss with two other shots aimed at her husband sleeping on the other side? The fact that the killer was using an illegal silencer on the gun made the circumstances even more startling. The only suspect was a man seen lurking at the Kalajzich home on 11 January, but already the Police had their radar set on someone right in front of them. Someone with a both a motive, and opportunity and who had asked media to give him and his family time to grieve in private, it was Megan's husband, Andrew Kalajzich.

But all this would unfold sometime in the future. In the first week of February, there was coverage of the aftermath of NASA's *Challenger* disaster, which claimed the lives of seven astronauts shortly after take-off the previous week; the probe launched into the failed takeover of the Sydney Swans AFL club by high-profile doctor Geoffrey Edelstein and the success of Neville Wran's Labor Government in three NSW by-elections. At that time, the band Dire Straits had launched a three-month tour of Australian and New Zealand, including an unprecedented 16-night stretch of concerts in Sydney, on the back of their successful *Brothers in Arms* album. In movie theatres and at local drive-in theatres, *Back to the Future*, starring a young Michael J. Fox, was breaking box-office records. On Tuesday, the one-day cricket carnival rolled back into Sydney with Australia taking on India before the best of three finals were scheduled against the Kiwis.

It was the end of a fairly typical Australian summer, with most people already back at work after the summer break. All that was to change, of course, with the discovery of a young woman's body in a non-descript paddock in Sydney's west.

* * *

In 1986, there were approximately 200,000 people in the greater Blacktown area, with 75% of the population born in Australia (the next highest birthplace was the United Kingdom and Ireland, with 7%) with a 97.5% of the population speaking English as their first language. 68% of the populace had no trade or qualification, with 6% having a trade and only 4.5% having a diploma or higher education. More than 50% of the population earned more than $10,000 a year, with the median income between $18,000 and $22,000 per year. About 50% of the population was under 30 years of age.

A century before, Blacktown had been an Aboriginal settlement, from which it took its name – literally the 'black's' town – some 35 kilometres west of the Sydney CBD. Its main claim to fame before 1986 was that it was the venue for Labor leader Gough Whitlam's famous 'It's Time' campaign that would take him all the way to the Prime Ministership of Australia in 1972. The suburb, like many in low socio-economic areas, would be hardest hit by the recession the Whitlam government oversaw during the 1970s and again under Fraser in the early 1980s. In the decades that followed, Blacktown would often seek to shrug off its colonial past and rename the city – some even suggested Whitlam, but the names of former prime ministers are reserved for the suburbs of Canberra – so debate still wages from time to time.

West of Blacktown is an enclave of satellite suburbs built around the traditional rail stop of Mt Druitt. Bidwell, Blackett, Emerton, Hebersham, Shalvey, Tregear, Whalan and Willmott, with Rooty Hill, Lethbridge Park and Doonside close to Blacktown. There were problems of course, with an abundance of housing commission dwellings attracting low income families with associated issues of poor education and poor job prospects.

Symptomatic of the many issues the suburb faced was an incident in Bidwell in October 1981. Dozens of teenagers attracted national attention when they brawled in the streets in front of a crowd of 1000 people. The children later claimed they were 'bored' … this attracted a response from the NSW Neville Wran Government which built three new youth centres.

It was a drop in the well of disaffection and disillusionment.

'There are areas of Mt Druitt, really nice streets and we never had to go there for a job. There are so many great people down there,' says former Detective Tom Sharp, who was in charge of the Mt Druitt detectives in the 1980s, and a colleague to many of the men who investigated the Anita Cobby case. After spending nine years with the vice squad, Sharp spent several months at Blacktown in 1986 before shifting to 'The Druitt'. 'Some of the families, however, you were there all the time. You didn't need a warrant because the mother would just let you in. "Would you mind if we had a look through?" we'd ask.'

'At one stage there were only a handful of homes that hadn't been broken into in Chestnut Crescent (Bidwill)… and that was because the people in those homes were basically the offenders. All the street signs in the local area had been stolen … the thinking being if the police couldn't find their way through the area they couldn't catch you.

Most of the arrests were for break and enters, stolen motor vehicles, sexual assaults and, every now and again, a siege for domestic issues', says Sharp. 'We would investigate four or five murders a year, and they would take up a lot of our investigation time. Often, our superiors would want to curb your overtime to make it look good on the books and I used to say "What price is a life? What price is a murder?"'

When Sharp returned Mt Druitt in 1986, the drug trade was fairly-well entrenched, which resulted in break and enters going up. 'We were having 300 break and enters a month, which was huge,' he recalls. 'I organised with people from the fingerprint section to come out to the station and every time we caught somebody we'd take them before the court and hold them over for ten days and fingerprint them. For six weeks, we collected every available fingerprint sample from break and enters and stolen vehicles.'

After a while the fingerprint database was getting five or six hits at a time. 'The Druitt had a bad name,' says Sharp. 'I had a talk with the local press and suggested that when there was a crime not to call it Mt Druitt, but name the actual suburb. They said they couldn't do that because no one knew where the suburbs were and it would be bad reporting.'

'The privately-run post office at Mt Druitt had nine armed holdups,' Sharp remembers. 'There was a bit of grass there, but harder drugs were coming in. When I came back in the 1980s, the drug scene was full on … amphetamines and heroin. Amphetamines were prescribed as a weight-loss pill in the 1980s and offenders would 'doctor shop' for medication scripts.' These were the days before computerisation and the linking of data bases between chemists.

Retired Blacktown Detective Sergeant Graham Rosetta agrees it was a tough area to police. 'In Blacktown and Mt Druitt, there was a vast population of unemployed adults and youths. A lack of education, poor socio-economic circumstances and unemployment were some of the elements that fuelled local crime. I also don't think they had as many support services as they have now.'

Offenders in the 16–25 year old age group were highly represented in crime figures … in saying that, a lot injury and disadvantage was self-inflicted because of the poor choices that were made.

In his classic 'novelisation' of the factual murder of a Kansas family, 'In Cold Blood', American writer Truman Capote talks of the collision of two worlds … one 'desperate, ruthless, wandering and savage' and the other 'insular and safe'. Those two worlds, in the neighbouring suburbs of Doonside and Blacktown, were to collide in Western Sydney on Sunday night, 2 February, 1986.

The murder of Anita Cobby captured public attention like few others and still resonates in the psyche of Western Sydney.

CHAPTER TWO

The Crime

About midday on Tuesday, two days after Anita Cobby had gone missing, Detectives Ian Kennedy and Garry Heskett knocked on the Lynches' door in Sullivan Street, Blacktown. They politely asked Garry Lynch, Anita's father, to come outside before telling him a body had been found in a local paddock … and it could be that of his missing daughter. 'I saw a void,' Garry Lynch later reflected, 'and I was too scared to think what that void might hold.'

At about 8am on Tuesday, 2 February 1986, dairy farmer John Reen left his home in Prospect, on the southern side of the Great Western Highway adjacent to the suburb of the Western Sydney suburb of Blacktown, to attend the Camden cattle sales. As he drove along Reen Road, a dirt track named after the family property, and towards a 'boiler paddock' used to graze cattle unsuitable for consumption, he observed some of his cows milling around a corner of the paddock. When he returned home shortly before lunch, the cows were still there, which the farmer thought was unusual. After attending a few chores around his homestead, he decided to ride his motorbike about 600 metres down to the spot and check it out.

That's when the 44-year-old dairy farmer discovered the naked body of a woman lying on the ground. The cows had licked the body clean of blood in an attempt to soak up all the salt in the heat of the day. Reen rang Blacktown Police Station and told the young constable on the other end of the phone, 'you better send some blokes up to my property … there's a body of a girl in one of them.'

Reen Road was soon a hive of activity as local detectives and uniformed police sealed off the crime scene – a clearing of long grass between a large grey tree and a black stump. 'I thought it was a doll,' Reen later told the media crews that descended on his home. 'I couldn't believe it was a body.' Shortly after midday, detectives from Sydney CIB's Homicide Squad arrived at the scene.

At the time, Garry Heskett was a Detective Constable First Class, a ranking that no longer exists in NSW. Heskett had worked at Blacktown for three and a half years before moving into Homicide CIB in the city. 'I received a phone call from Superintendent Wally Hendricks, the commander at Penrith,' he recalls. 'Wally knew me and I knew him, so the phone call started with the usual courtesies before he said, "Ah young Garry, being an old Blacktown boy you're just the guy I want to talk to."'

Ian 'Speed' Kennedy was a Detective Sergeant in the Homicide Squad. 'We were on a roster; the next murder that came up, you got it,' Kennedy says matter-of-factly. 'It could have been Broken Hill, Albury or Bondi. The normal procedure in those days was when there was a murder, the local detective sergeant would notify Homicide. They would start the investigation and spend two to three days on it, identifying suspects and trying to reach a solution. If there were problems, they would bring in a team from Homicide, two or four detectives according to their availability, to help solve the crime.

'In this case, because there was a body of a girl in a paddock and they didn't know who she was at this stage, they decided to call Homicide and send a team straight out. A place as small as Blacktown Police Station couldn't afford to have four of five detectives working on the one murder for three or four months because there was so much other crime in the area to deal with, and with other court and work commitments.'

'I went out there with Garry Heskett, who wasn't my partner (my regular partner was on holidays and his partner Kevin Raue had the day off.) The beauty was, Garry and Kevin had worked at Blacktown before.'

Heskett was soon back in well-known territory, surrounded by familiar faces from the Blacktown Police Station. Detectives Graham Rosetta and Hugh Dundas had been called in from their rostered days off to attend the scene. They were soon joined by Detectives Paul Dundas, Phil Gaspert, Chris O'Toole and John Wakefield, the latter detective on his final day at Blacktown before being transferred to Penrith. Two more detectives, Tony Waters and Garry Raymond, would join the team when they returned to Sydney the following day.

Detective Sergeant Graham Rosetta, the most senior of the Blacktown detectives, was one of the first on the scene. 'It was obvious from the beginning that more than one person was involved in the murder,' he says. 'The fact that the poor woman was carried so far over a fence and into a paddock would have been no mean feat even for one man.'

Kennedy and Heskett were briefed by local detectives as they walked over to a clearing and observed the naked body of a young female lying on her stomach in a kneeling position. Her head was positioned on her arm, her legs were slightly apart and there were a number of scratches and bruises on her back. There were cuts to her hands, indicative of defensive words, and several fingers were cut and broken. Two large lacerations to her neck were also visible, the severity of which became evident to the two detectives when the body was gently rolled over.

'One did not have to be Sherlock Holmes to realise that the cutting of the throat was the final act of the attack and that the victim resisted to the bitter end in an effort to stop the knife cutting her throat,' says Heskett. The brutality of the crime was sickening even to the most hardened police officer. 'If you were not emotionally affected by the gravity of the act then one could not be described as human in the true sense.'

'We scoured the paddock for evidence and found nothing,' Ian Kennedy says. There were no clothes, no bag and no identification at the crime scene, just a large quantity of blood on the ground and patches of cow manure where the cows had been milling. Pol Air, the Police Rescue Squad, trail bike and dog squad and uniformed police were joined by hundreds of cadets from Goulburn Police Academy in the search.

'I knew the boss of the Goulburn Academy, so I phoned him and said he had a readymade force down there and it would be a good experience to get the cadets up here and get them to take part in the search. "Not a problem," he said, and so up they came on a bus and I briefed them what we were looking for and how to go about it. As soon as something was found, the line had to stop.'

It was to be a meticulous forensic search, but still nothing was found at the scene relating to the crime.

John Reen, the farmer who first found the body, informed the police that over the weekend, either on Saturday or Sunday night, he had heard loud screams coming from the area. Reen Road was an isolated area, however, commonly used as a 'lovers' lane'. Blacktown Drive-In was not too far away and young hoons would go down to the deserted road for drinking sessions and the occasional drag race, so Reen thought nothing more of the screams he'd heard at the time.

As the temperature continued to climb that day, Dr Joe Malouf, the Government Medical Officer, arrived along with Detective Senior Constable Paul Hamilton of the Penrith Scientific Branch. A detailed examination of the crime scene ensued and the body of the young woman and the surrounding area was photographed.

Ian Kennedy says: 'The eyes were open, which is not unusual in a murder; there was blood around the mouth, her nose was broken, and contusions and swelling around the eye. There were lots of marks on the body … a bite mark or gouge, a large bruise on the body was from a kick. Someone had dragged her through the barbed wire fence of the paddock … then there were the broken fingers and defensive wounds where she had grabbed the blade during the attack. You can only imagine the fear and pain she went through.'

The detectives were still examining the body when a Constable Murphy arrived from Blacktown Station with a missing persons' report. Murphy had taken the report from local man Garry Lynch the previous day after his 29-year-old daughter Anita had failed to return home from work on Sunday night. Constable Murphy had a photo of the missing woman in his hand. He informed the detectives that he had gone to school with Anita in the late 1970s, but the body in front of him was so badly beaten he couldn't tell if it was her or not. The experienced detectives, however, had no doubt the body of the young woman in front of them was the missing woman.

The next step in the investigation was the formal identification of the victim. Under the watchful eye of Dr Malouf, Ian Kennedy removed gold interlocking Russian wedding rings from the victim's right hand for possible identification purposes. The rings were secured in a plastic bag, and Kennedy and Heskett made the short journey to the Lynch household in South Blacktown.

Garry Heskett remembers the car ride to Sullivan Street as a quiet one, both detectives knowing the difficult task that lay ahead … informing the family that their daughter was dead and then having the couple identify her body. 'All the police training in the world never seems to prepare one for those dark and sorrowful occasions,' Heskett says. 'The Lynches were very decent people. When 'Speed' Kennedy and I went out to the Lynch household in Blacktown, I said that we don't need to be there any longer than necessary. It was very tough.'

When Kennedy and Heskett knocked on the door in Sullivan Street, they were greeted by Garry and Grace Lynch, a suburban couple in their 60s, alongside their youngest daughter Kathryn and her husband Ray Eedens. 'All we could say to the Lynches at that stage was that a deceased female had been located in a paddock and the body resembled his daughter,' says Heskett.

'I'll always remember Garry's reply,' Kennedy says. '"I wish I could say it wasn't but then it would be someone else's daughter," he said. "They would then have to go through what we're going through." Although we didn't come out and say it then, I feel deep down the Lynches knew in their hearts that their daughter had been located.'

When Ian Kennedy showed Garry the wedding rings taken from the victim's hand, Garry wasn't sure they were his daughter's rings. It was 20-year-old Kathryn who confirmed that it was her sister's wedding ring, asking the detectives why it was 'dirty and rusty'.

There wasn't rust on the ring, Kennedy explained. It was blood.

The detectives made brief enquiries about the missing daughter's clothing and her last known movements. The Lynches hugged each other and cried.

Garry Heskett says, 'I sensed we were invading in their private moment. Soon they would be asking questions we weren't in a position to answer, being so early in the investigation. They were looking at us with piercing eyes ... looking straight through you like an x-ray searching for answers. Why did this happen to their daughter? And we didn't have too many answers for them then. We needed to get some information and get out of there and start our work.'

After they obtained a number of recent photographs of Anita, Kennedy and Heskett left for Blacktown Police Station. Later that afternoon they returned to the Lynch home and spoke to John Cobby, Anita's estranged husband. The two detectives found the young man sitting on the back step of the Lynch home, inconsolable. He formally identified the wedding rings as the ones belonging to Anita.

Kennedy and Heskett discussed with the family the need to formally identify the body. They both believed Garry Lynch was the stronger of the parents and should identify the body. Grace Lynch wanted to attend the mortuary with her husband, but was dissuaded by the detectives who told her it was best she remember her daughter 'the way she was in life'. John Cobby could not face the task, so Garry Lynch and Ray, Garry's other son-in-law at the time, went to Westmead Morgue with the detectives.

Grace Lynch later maintained that she should have been allowed to go to the morgue to support her husband when he needed her. Anita was her daughter too, she said. Whether it would have helped or not, she didn't know, but she was a nursing sister and had given birth to Anita. She wanted to be there.

At the morgue, Garry was taken into a small room and stood before a glass window and curtain. When the curtain was drawn open, he saw his daughter's lifeless body on the other side of the glass.

'(Garry) looked like he was going to collapse and his knees buckled,' Garry Heskett remembers. 'I put my arm around him and pulled him in to comfort and console him … he straightened up and wiped away his tears.'

'Is that your daughter, Garry?' the detectives asked. He could only lower his head and nod. His daughter's features had changes, her face was swollen and her teeth were crooked, but there was no mistaking her thick, curly black hair and the general outline of her face.

'They uncovered her face and I saw that she looked perfectly peaceful,' Garry Lynch would write a decade later. 'I didn't know then the horror of how she died because there was no evidence of that. She was covered up very neatly with a high collared blouse.'

With the help of his son-in-law, Garry was escorted back to the car by the two detectives and was taken home to Sullivan Street. After the shock of identifying his daughter's body, the detectives kept Garry's mind active by outlining what would happen next. 'We talked about the case and the strategies that are usually instigated in matters like this,' Garry Heskett says. 'We also warned him to prepare for the inevitable intrusion of the media that will soon be trampling over each other to beat a path to his door.'

When Garry Lynch arrived home and he delivered the news to the rest of the family, they just held each other and cried. 'You should be proud of your daughter,' Garry remembers the detectives telling them. 'She fought like a tiger.'

Later that evening, the two detectives took Garry Lynch to the boiler paddock where Anita's body had been found earlier that day. Although Kennedy told him it sounded like a cruel thing to do, he knew from his experience as a homicide detective that it would also help the grieving father come to terms with his loss. Kennedy and Heskett showed him the exact place where they found her body. 'Near a dead old stump tree,' Garry Lynch later commented, 'and it helped me to know. There was no more mystery.'

Lynch noticed the blood on the ground, and he later said a part of him wanted 'to scoop that up and take that home' with him. All he could do was 'just look at it and know what it was … [and] go away with a heavy heart.'

Later, they would take Grace Lynch there too, and it did help her to come to terms with the reality of it all, but it provided few answers for them both.

But a stark question had already formed in the minds of the detectives working on the case, in each and every uniformed and cadet policeman at the crime scene, and also in the Lynch family and their circle of friends. Following the evening television reports and the arrival of morning newspapers the following day, the same question would germinate in thousands of Sydney-ites and gradually take seed in the entire nation.

Who could do such a thing to another human being?

CHAPTER THREE

The Victim

Grace: Anita was a beautiful person. She'd grown up into a beautiful young lady. She didn't always want to be a nurse but she wanted to do something with her life … and she really enjoyed it … really loved it.

Garry: Anita was the quintessence of dignity.

Grace: She was happy ... she was just a nice person.

Graham McNeice Interview, 2005.

On Tuesday, 4 February 1986, State Coroner Derrick Hand was informed that the body of a young woman had been found in a paddock in Western Sydney. It was believed to be that of a young nurse who went missing while walking home to her parents' house in Blacktown on Sunday night. Garry Lynch would formally identify the body as belonging to his eldest daughter Anita later that day.

At Westmead Morgue, the body was photographed and then washed to reveal the full extent of the bruising and injuries. Anita Cobby had died from the result of massive blood loss after her throat had been cut, Chief Medical Officer Dr Joe Malouf would write. There were three major cuts to her body, as well as three minor cuts and numerous scratches and abrasions.

There were two major cuts to her throat, the second of which cut her from ear to ear (from right to left), cutting through the major organs, tissue and nerves, and almost severing the head. The second cut was also on the right side of the throat, which in itself would have been fatal, and a third cut was to the cheek of the right side of the face. This wound was consistent with the point of a large knife being held against the victim's face.

There were also cuts to the fingers, consistent with defensive wounds. A series of marks on her back and legs had clearly been made when she was naked and indicated she was forcibly pulled through a barbed wire fence. Post mortem results showed a large number of very deep bruises inflicted upon her by heavy blows from punches or kicks. There was a large bruise to her hip, consistent with a kick when she was on the ground, as well as bruising and barbed wire punctures under her left arm.

The victim had also been raped multiple times, and there were cuts and abrasions to her anus. Because of the large amount of blood on the ground where her body was found, the doctor was of the opinion that her neck had been cut from behind, starting at one ear and slicing and hacking across the throat, causing blood to spurt from her neck. The woman was conscious until the moment her throat was cut, so she knew what was going to happen to her that night, heightening the horror of it all, if that was even possible.

Dr Malouf estimated it would have taken the victim two full minutes to die.

* * *

Anita Lorraine Lynch was born on 2 November 1959. The eldest daughter of Garry and Grace 'Peg' Lynch, the family was living in the Inner Sydney suburb of Glebe at the time but moved to Blacktown soon after. Anita's childhood was full of the things Western Sydney kids typically experience – softball, Girl Guides, music and art. She attended Walters Road Public School in Blacktown and later Evans High School where she completed her HSC in 1977. As a teenager she developed other interests like going to the beach. Her father later observed, 'And she loved dances. And ironing her hair straight … '

Neighbour Anne King suggested Anita enter the NSW Spastic Centre's Miss Australia Quest. Anne's son Martin King had dated Anita during their teenage years, and she was close to the Lynch family. The Miss Australia Quest was not really a beauty contest so much as a way of raising funds for the handicapped. The winner was usually the best ambassador for the cause, not necessarily the prettiest. Anita just happened to be both.

Anita and her family spent most of the 1979–80 year selling raffle tickets in Parramatta Mall and raising $10,000. At a formal ceremony at the Wentworth Hotel in 1980, Anita beat 56 other contestants to be proclaimed Miss Western Suburbs. She was awarded a sash and a tiara from the NSW Attorney General Frank Walker and his wife. 'She was a very popular girl with the younger and older generations and had loads of personality,' Anne King remembers. 'She had finally found something that she could contribute to the world. She just loved helping people.'

Anita had 'great empathy for others' her parents said, an inner beauty as well as an external beauty. 'Anita was a superb model,' Garry Lynch wrote. 'She had a wonderful deportment down the catwalk and a beautiful figure for all the clothes that were presented for her to wear – a delight to watch.'

Although she missed out on the Miss New South Wales title at the next stage of competition, Anita was rewarded with a trip to Hawaii with the other girls. When she came home from Hawaii, she told her parents she was 'so glad be out of that plastic world.' She tried her hand at modelling for Westfield's shopping centres but that meant little to her, the Lynches said, and the notion of helping others was resonating with her. After spending a year in an office job, Anita decide d to apply to Goulburn Police Academy. Anita's mother was a nurse, and although the idea of a nursing career had originally repulsed her ('Yuk, blood, bedpans!') Anita also decided to enrol in a nursing degree at Sydney Hospital.

It was there Anita met her future husband, fellow nurse John Cobby. They married in March 1982, and when they lived in Sydney they owned a 35-foot yacht, which they sailed on Sydney Harbour.

According to Garry Lynch, they sold the boat when they moved to Coffs Harbour to work in a private hospital, but John Cobby was also heavily involved in horse racing and the pair started to drift apart. In 1985, the Cobbys spent four months overseas travelling but when they returned to Australia their marriage was in real trouble. Shortly before Christmas 1985, Anita returned to her family home in Blacktown.

In early 1986, Anita Cobby's marriage was over and she was working as an intensive care nurse in Sydney. She was making plans to find a flat to share with a girlfriend. She wanted to travel, she had taken up painting again and she was keen to take Spanish lessons. She planned to do another nursing degree at Sydney Hospital. Anita Cobby had a lot of plans for the future.

On Friday, 31 January 1986, Anita and her father spent the day together while Grace Lynch worked at a local nursing home. Anita had bought some watercolour paints and art paper and drew two seashells. Garry, a former commercial artist with the Navy, showed her a picture of a leatherjacket which she copied to complete the picture. Anita skilfully drew the leatherjacket attacking a sea urchin and added a group of four shells 'radiating five points.'

Garry remarked that it was a lovely picture and Anita said it was symbolic of 'the Age of Aquarius' .... the start of a golden millennium, she said, a thousand years of love and peace.

The following day, Anita went to work at Sydney Hospital, but did not get home until well after midnight. The train had taken her to Yagoona, on the southern district line, because the western route was closed for maintenance works. She had to get up early for work the following morning to start at 7am and was annoyed her train had taken her miles out of her way. But what could she do?

Grace stated, 'The previous night, I think she got a taxi, because she came home late and she was a bit upset because she had trouble with the train. She was about an hour getting home and she was concerned about that. She said that she hoped that she didn't have to start living out this way because it was too far for her.'

Early on Sunday morning, Garry was still in bed when he heard Anita and Grace talking over breakfast. He listened as the front door opened and shut, and he heard his daughter's footsteps going down the path. 'I was never to say goodbye to her,' he said, 'a fact I was to regret often.'

Sunday, 2 February 1986, was the hottest for that calendar day on record, 38.7 degrees (or 100°F on the old scale). That day, Anita worked at Sydney Hospital from 7.00am to 3.30pm. In the evening she went out for dinner with friends Lyn Bradshaw and Elaine Bray at a Lebanese restaurant in Elizabeth Street, Redfern. Anita told her friends she would catch a train from Central Station shortly after 9pm in order to return to Blacktown. She had to work another shift the next day.

Lyn Bradshaw dropped Anita off at the Eddy Avenue entrance to Central Station in time for her to catch the 9:12pm train to Blacktown. 'We asked her to stay with one of us for the night instead of going all the way to Blacktown,' Miss Bradshaw said. 'She said "See you tomorrow" and I went home ...'

It was the last time she would see her friend alive.

Since returning to live at her parents' home in Blacktown, Anita would either catch a taxi from Blacktown Station or ring her father Garry from a phone box across from the station to come and pick her up after working late. On this particular night, however, there were no taxis available and the public phone booths had been vandalised and weren't working. With daylight saving still in operation, the night was warm and still. Anita made the decision to walk home to Sullivan Street, some three kilometres to the southwest of the station, which she would cover in about 40 minutes.

When Anita Cobby did not arrive home that night, her parents Garry and Grace assumed that their daughter had stayed in the city with friends. Grace later recalled, 'It was a very hot night and she got to the station and there probably weren't any taxis available and she decided to walk home and why can't we walk on our footpath? She had done it before … '

On Monday, Grace went off to work at the local nursing home around midday. When Sydney Hospital rang the Lynch home to enquire why Anita had not turned up for her rostered shift, Garry Lynch instinctively knew something wasn't right. Anita never let anyone down. Something was wrong.

'That was my first moment of misgiving because Anita was a person of absolute punctuality and dedication,' Garry Lynch later wrote. The hospital told him they had spoken to her work friends from the previous night, and they said she had caught a train home about 9pm. 'That's when I really started to go down.'

Grace suggested that Garry go straight to Blacktown Police Station and report their daughter was missing. The young constable who took the report, Constable Murphy, remarked that he knew Anita when she had been a few years ahead of him at Evans High School, a coincidence sharpened by the fact his surname – one that would leave an indelible mark on the Lynch family for years to come – had an irony of its own, not yet revealed.

Constable Murphy told Mr Lynch that there was nothing that could be done for 48 hours, as was standard operational procedure in missing persons' cases, but he would put out an all-points bulletin. 'This was not an unusual course of action,' says Garry Heskett, 'because of her age, the fact that she had recently separated and sometimes stayed with friends in the bush on a whim.' But her family were increasingly worried because it was so out of character for Anita not to ring them and let them know where she was.

Grace Lynch came home from work at 9pm that night and she and her husband were joined by their daughter Kathryn, Kathryn's husband Ray and Anita's estranged husband John Cobby. When he was told Anita was missing, John left a dinner engagement straight away. The family spent the evening contacting family and friends, but no one had seen her.

John Cobby was on the way to Wollongong to search for Anita among groups of friends on the south coast when he heard that a young woman's body had been found in a paddock on Reen Road, not far from his in-laws' house. He immediately turned his car around and headed there. Later that evening, the worst would be confirmed.

It was Anita.

When a tearful matron at Sydney Hospital broke the news to the medical staff, Anita's friend Lyn Bradshaw was screaming before the words came out of her mouth.

CHAPTER FOUR

THE INVESTIGATION

'We had a group of "street talk suspects" and often it's very accurate. I spoke to a lot of women in the area about who would do such a thing to a girl like Anita Cobby and the names of the offenders did come up … the Murphy brothers, and Travers, but not Murdoch that much … he was something of an unknown who linked in with Travers.'
'One guy reported "John Travers is a deviant … if any person was killed like that it would be him." The street talks and the street knows.'
Former detective, Garry Raymond

During the first week of the murder investigation, media attention escalated as the facts of the case slowly unfolded … a Sydney nurse walking home from work had been raped and murdered. How could this have happened? With so few leads, the media was looking for any angle possible. Detective Sergeant Ian Kennedy recalled, 'I would have a press conference at nine o'clock to tie up any loose ends and update any leads the Blacktown police had, but I would get phone calls from members of the press from 5am wanting a scoop … "was there anything I had to report?"'

One news agency discovered a photo of NSW Premier Neville Wran serving morning tea to Anita Cobby and some other girls during her beauty quest days in 1979. 'The media actually embarrassed Wran,' Kennedy recalls. 'The press asked him what was happening with the Cobby murder and he didn't know who they were talking about. And then they showed Wran the photo of him and Anita as Miss Western Suburbs. He was shocked … he had forgotten all about her.'

The NSW Government quickly posted a $50,000 reward. 'This is just one of the foulest crimes of the century and the animals responsible must be brought to justice,' Neville Wran told the Sydney press. The State government and the police hierarchy wanted the case solved … and fast.

'I got a phone call out at Blacktown from headquarters saying I had to brief them at 9am every morning and 4pm every afternoon,' recalls Kennedy. 'I told them to get stuffed, I wasn't doing that. "I'm too busy at nine o'clock and I'm too busy at four o'clock to do that," I told them. That just doesn't happen in a murder inquiry. Things have to be kept "in house" … how did I know information was not going to get leaked to the press?'

Kennedy offered a compromise. 'I tell you what I will do,' he said to his superiors. 'I'll let you know once I have anything of any real importance to report. If not, all you have to say to the media is that there is no change and the investigation is continuing.' The inspector was a mate of mine from my class at the academy, so he agreed. "I will cover for you but it might come undone," he said.

'If it comes undone I'll take the blame,' Kennedy told him.

Sometimes, however, the press went too far. At the end of a tense week, outspoken 2GB radio broadcaster John Laws hit the airwaves.

NSW State Coroner Derrick Hand was listening in his car as he drove to work at the end of a hot and hectic week. 'I am not easily roused to anger but I was furious as I listened to John Laws in disbelief,' he later observed. 'He was reading out the details of Anita Cobby's post mortem. Goodness knows where he got it from because, as a matter of course, details of a post mortem are never given out to the media. Apart from protecting the family's privacy, the report may also reveal details which the police need to catch whoever was responsible … someone had let us down by leaking the details.'

Laws told his radio audience that he would be telling his listeners other details the following Monday. 'Not if I had anything to do with it,' the Coroner maintained.

Hand instructed the Crown solicitor to contact Laws, and the remainder of the report was not read out by him or anyone else. 'Laws claimed he had been acting in the public interest,' Hand observed. 'While it was probably interesting to the public, this is not the definition of it being in the "public interest". In my view, it was just sensationalism.'

Ian Kennedy's role as Officer in Charge was to coordinate the investigation and to provide information and seek public assistance through the large media contingent on hand, and most importantly, to check all incoming information reports as they came in and were actioned by those detectives on the case. The team of 16 detectives was broken into mini-teams: one group was responsible for interviewing all known sex offenders living in the Blacktown area. Another had to respond to information offered up by the public. One team had to eliminate all taxi drivers working in the area, which involved interviewing all the owners and drivers and checking taxi radio logs. Two years before, a young woman had been abducted and murdered by a taxi driver after a night out, so that possibility had to be ruled out.

Most homicide investigations start from the inside out. One team had to interview all of Anita's family, friends and workmates to see if anyone had a motive to harm the young nurse. When John Cobby was asked as a matter of course if he killed his ex-wife, he burst into tears and literally fell apart. Cobby was quickly ruled out as a suspect, but there was more pain along the way for the Lynch family. Detectives had to ask Grace and Garry whether their daughter was promiscuous, was she a drug user, did she have any known enemies? In his grief, Garry Lynch later said that in the initial investigation he suspected everyone and anyone who had ever come into contact with his daughter.

The police needed to determine what happened to Anita after she left Blacktown Station. The first breakthrough in the case came a couple of days into the investigation when Detective Constable Paul Davies decided to recheck the telephone logs at Blacktown Station for the night of 2 February. Had anyone reported anything to police that night?

'He came upstairs and plonked the report down in front of me and said, "Get a load of that,"' says Garry Heskett.

On Sunday night, teenager Linda McGaughey was watching TV at home on Newton Road, Blacktown, at about 9.50pm when she heard a woman scream. Running out onto her driveway, she saw 'a dirty white-looking car' across Newton Road with a man in the back passenger side. 'At the same time, I also saw a female being pulled into the back seat by this man,' she told detectives. 'He had hold of her by one of her arms and by the shoulder. The vehicle was stationary, with the back passenger door open. I could see that this female was trying to struggle free by pulling backwards.'

The woman was screaming … a 'frightened scream,' Linda elaborated. 'Very frightened and very loud.' The roadway was not that well lit, but she clearly saw a woman being forced into the rear seat of a light coloured, early model Holden sedan.

Linda called for her older brother John, who was at the back of the house, but by the time he came out, the woman had been bundled into the car. As John McGaughey ran towards the car, the rear door of the vehicle closed and it drove off, turning left into Walters Road. The McGaughey siblings were unsure of the model of Holden the men were driving and did not see the number plate of the car, but they could see there were at least two men involved.

A short time later, their 19-year-old brother Paul McGaughey returned home with his girlfriend after a night out. When Linda explained to him that a young woman had been dragged into a Holden, Paul and his girlfriend drove off in his car and searched for the vehicle while John contacted Blacktown Police Station. Instinctively, Paul ended up at Reen Road, a well-known local hang-out, and noticed a number of cars at the end of the dirt road. One car, a grey-coloured Holden, fit the general description of the car he was looking for but when he shone a light on the car, it was empty. He continued the search, not realising how close he had come to the crime scene.

The task force still had precious little to go on. The police were confident that Anita was the female abducted on Newton Road and, because of what the eyewitness had said and the extent of her injuries, they knew more than one person was involved. If she had walked home from Blacktown Station, Newton Road would be on the route. A train had arrived at Blacktown at about 9.40pm that night, so the timing suggested that it was Anita who was abducted walking home. Detectives asked for anyone who had seen Anita on that train that night to come forward and the train guard on the 9:12 from Central was adamant that she had caught that train.

During the week, police decided they would conduct a re-enactment of Anita's last movements on the night she died. At the time, Debbie Wallace was one of only two uniformed constables attached to the General Duties section of Blacktown Police Station. When Detective Sergeant Kevin Raue asked to have a word with the young constable, Wallace was flattered; she was roughly the same age and physically resembled Anita. The plan was to dress Wallace in clothing approximating what Anita wore on the night she was abducted and retrace the young nurse's final journey from Sydney by train and on the streets of Blacktown a week after Anita disappeared.

This re-enactment would allow the police to approximate the time of the journey, and Wallace's appearance as 'Anita' might prompt members of the public to remember something about that night. Although it was decided the media would have to be involved because coverage might encourage someone to come forward, Wallace did not expect the swarm of pressmen and television cameras that greeted her on the Eddy Avenue forecourt at Central Station on the night of the re-enactment. It was a media frenzy.

In the days before the re-enactment, Wallace went shopping with Anita's friends who had dined with her that night. They selected pale pink ski pants, a white top and flat white shoes, items they believed were similar to those Anita wore on the night she disappeared. Wallace caught the 9:12pm train to Blacktown, with media contingent in tow. Leaving the train at Blacktown Station, she stopped on the shopping centre side of the railway while the media snapped away. Leaving the media behind, but trailed by a car of detectives, Wallace began her walk along the likely route suggested by the investigators.

The strategy resulted in an unbelievable public response. When Anita was cremated at Pine Grove Crematorium on Monday, 10 February, the Lynches gave permission for the media to attend their most private moment of grieving – the police had asked for them to be there. The perpetrator of the crime often comes and mingles with the mourners, detectives told Garry and Grace Lynch, and the media coverage would help get the message out to the public.

But the police had already received information from a number of people that a Doonside teenager named John Travers was a person capable of this type of murder and that he was known to carry a knife. Some said he cut the throats of sheep from ear to ear as a 'party trick' in an eerily similar manner to the wound inflicted on Anita Cobby. Travers, then aged only 18, was wanted for the rape of a young girl on 8 January that year. Police later learned that he was also wanted by Western Australia Police for a sexual assault for which he had been arrested but had absconded on bail. The detectives were trying to locate him, but their best efforts had proved fruitless.

On 18 February, a criminal informant told the task force that Travers and another man named Michael Murdoch had stolen a beige green Holden from a Seven Hills home on 29 January, three days before the murder. They had changed the plates and spray-painted the vehicle undercoat grey. The mag wheels and sheepskin seat covers had allegedly been given to a Lesley Murphy who had put them on his Holden station wagon.

Finding that car was now paramount to tying it to the abduction and murder of Anita Cobby. The car had been abandoned on Plumpton Road on the outskirts of Blacktown and then, on Friday, 7 February, burnt out. A Blacktown City Council ordinance inspector had made a note of an abandoned car on Plumpton Road and recorded the license plate and engine numbers but when he returned the car had disappeared. The car had been dumped and burnt out, which was peculiar given the thieves had gone to the trouble of repainting it. Were they hiding something?

On Friday 21 February, police conducted a series of raids in Western Sydney in an effort to locate John Travers and the stolen car. Police went to Travers' family home in Tich Place, Doonside, some five kilometres west of where Anita Cobby had been taken from Newton Road. They found Les Murphy living there with Travers' teenage sister in a caravan at the back of the home. Murphy's car was fitted with mag wheels and sheepskin seats, which the 23-year-old said were his. Police were able identify the wheels and seat covers as belonging to the stolen Holden because their owner had engraved his initials on the wheel rims.

Detectives described Murphy as 'a tough little character' but 'very nervous' when they questioned him. Graham Rosetta later stated, 'We asked if he'd heard about the murder up in Prospect and he said, "Yeah, I heard about it." Did he know John Travers? "Yes." Do you think he had anything to do with the murder? "No, he hasn't got it in him."'

Hours later, John Travers and Michael Murdoch were arrested in bed together at the home of Travers' uncle in Jewelsford Road, Wentworthville. Graham Rosetta told Travers that they were investigating the theft of a 1969 or 1970 Holden sedan that had been repainted with grey undercoat and the murder of Blacktown nurse named Anita Cobby.

'Wait a minute,' Travers protested. 'We knocked off a green HT, but we had nothing to do with the murder of the nurse.'

Rosetta searched the house and found a sheath knife under a mattress. When asked who owned the knife, Travers said he did. At the police station later that night, Rosetta showed Travers what appeared to be blood stains on the knife.

"I didn't cut that slut's throat,' was Travers' telling reply.

'I haven't suggested you did,' Rosetta said. 'Can you tell me if that is blood on the knife?

Travers said, 'Yes it is but it's not her blood, its sheep's blood.' When asked how he knew that, he volunteered, 'Because I killed a sheep in the backyard at home.'

Travers was charged with the theft of the car and kept in custody because he was wanted on a charge of rape. The manner of Travers' denial, given the fact that he owned a knife that could inflict such a wound on the victim, convinced Rosetta and the other detectives that the teenager was involved in the crime. Now all they had to do was prove it.

Michael Murdoch, also 18, admitted to Detective Sergeant Ian Kennedy that he had stolen a green HT Holden from outside a Seven Hills house on 29 January. He had done so, Murdoch told Kennedy, because he was asked to by Travers, who had 'a mate' who wanted a HT Holden. On the way to the Seven Hills home where he had stolen the car, Murdoch denied any knowledge of the murder of Anita Cobby. He claimed he was at Travers' Doonside home on the night of the murder, watching television with Mrs Travers and two of her sons. He could not recall which program he was watching but told Kennedy he watches 'a lot of TV'.

Interestingly, he did not offer Travers an alibi. Travers was not there that night.

Michael Murdoch was charged with stealing the car, but with nothing else to go on he was granted bail. Les Murphy was also charged and given bail. After the pair left Blacktown Police Station, they were placed under 24-hour surveillance.

The net was closing.

CHAPTER FIVE

The Informant

'We had a lot of circumstantial evidence but Miss X's evidence clinched it. It took Travers a while to get his head around the fact that he was gone ... he told Miss X everything because he trusted her and he gave up all the other people with him on that night [of the murder]. The basis of that trust was her acceptance of his behaviour in the past, and he thought she would blindly accept this behaviour as well. It was brilliant stuff; we couldn't believe what he told her.'

Former detective, Garry Raymond

On Saturday, 22 February, the day after John Travers was remanded on charges of car theft and sexual assault, Travers asked a cell sergeant to ring a family member to bring him cigarettes and clean underwear. Travers nominated his 'aunt', the de facto wife of his uncle, to run the errand for him. Detective Kevin Raue rang the woman, someone Travers trusted implicitly, and asked her to bring the items to Blacktown Station. The woman broke down on the phone. Could they meet in private? she sobbed. She had something to tell the detective but was too scared to come to the station.

The woman feared for her life.

Raue arranged to meet her that night, hoping that it was not a false lead. The task force had been inundated with a large number of calls and letters from clairvoyants, some saying they had 'seen it all happen in a dream' or that Anita was talking to them from the great beyond. Was this another dead end?

Raue met the woman in the carpark of Wentworthville League Club later that night. She told the detective she suspected Travers was responsible for the murder of Anita Cobby because he had told her of previous rapes and assaults in which he had used a large knife. Although the woman was a self-confessed heroin addict on a methadone program, she knew Travers well and knew what he was capable of. Nicknamed 'Trawney' by his mates, Travers treated females with 'utter contempt' and always carried a knife.

She also knew about a number of his rapes of young women, as well as a sexual assault in Western Australia, in which Travers had held a knife to the throat of a teenaged homosexual while he raped him from behind. Travers even had photos of the attack and showed them to her.

The day before he was arrested, Travers had told her things had gotten 'too hot' for him in Sydney and that he was heading 'up north, crocodile hunting'.

Raue encouraged the woman to come to Blacktown Police Station the following morning and speak to Travers at the door of his cell. When asked why she was 'giving up' Travers, she said that 'no woman should go through what that lady did. I don't care if they are prostitutes or druggies, no one should have that done to them.'

The detectives were amazed by the distinction she made.

Later, the woman's identity was supressed by the courts, and she was given the dramatic pseudonym 'Miss X' by NSW Coroner Derrick Hand. What she was able to get Travers to admit to would blow the case wide open. Detective Garry Heskett calls it the 'X-factor' of the investigation, the missing pieces of the puzzle that finally brought the men responsible for the crime into police focus.

At 9am on Sunday 23 February, Miss X spoke to Travers in a ground floor cell through a small grill in the door. Detective Raue stood at the end of the hallway, out of Travers' sight. 'It was imperative that she not ask him direct questions but simply react to what he said and to encourage further talk,' Ian Kennedy says. 'This was for two reasons: one, it might be construed by lawyers as coercion, trying to get him say certain things; and two, he might become suspicious and clam up.'

Miss X gave Travers the items he had requested and engaged him in conversation for about 15 minutes. In a rambling discussion in whispered tones, Travers told her that he had committed the murder of Anita Cobby and told her the names of the other four people involved … Michael Murdoch and the three Murphy brothers, Mick, Les and Gary.

When Miss X came out of the meeting with Travers, she collapsed in Raue's arms. Helped upstairs to where the detectives were waiting for her, she told them breathlessly, 'It's him; there were five of the bastards …' Travers had spoken to her of the brutal acts 'with sheer joy,' she said. 'He's not human.'

When she first came to his cell, Travers told her the police were trying to 'pin a murder' on him. 'I took hold of his hand and put it up against my face … tears were rolling down it,' Miss X said, adding that Travers too was starting to cry.

'I asked if he had done it and he said yes,' Miss X told the detectives. She asked Travers if there was anything else she could do to help him. Travers told her to contact Michael Murdoch and the Murphy brothers and get someone to find the burnt out stolen car and 'dump it in the river or cover it up.'

Although Travers had told Miss X the names of the others involved, including Mick and Gary Murphy, whom police did not know had been involved, there was no corroborating evidence. Both men were known to police. Mick Murphy, a 33-year-old convicted armed robber, was an escaped prisoner from Silverwater Gaol. His younger brother Gary, 28, had been involved in petty crime for most of his life but mainly car theft and receiving stolen goods. Abduction, rape and murder was a huge step up for both of them.

Kevin Raue was guarded. Was Travers big-noting himself or was it really because he wanted to get it all off his chest? 'Maybe he couldn't live with it anymore?' Raue later reflected. It was still Miss X's word against Travers'.

The detectives took a statement from Miss X, but they knew she would have to go back down to the cell with a listening device and get Travers' confession on tape. 'That way we would know she was telling the truth and would have his admissions legally on tape,' says Kennedy.

While Ian Kennedy prepared an application to obtain a listening device, on the instructions of detectives Miss X went to Travers' home in Tich Place, Doonside, at about 5.45pm. Miss X's partner, Travers' uncle, and their child, went with her to maintain an air of normalcy. There she met with six people, including Les Murphy, whom she did not know. Miss X told Murphy she had seen John Travers, who was holding up 'pretty good' in the cells. Travers, she said, wanted her to tell Murphy to find the stolen the car.

'We have to get rid of it,' she said Travers had ordered.

Les Murphy told Miss X that he would ring his sister and leave a message for his brothers who could then tell him the location of the car.

'They are after us for that murder,' Murphy told her, 'My sister wants me to go and stay with her.'

'Never mind about that,' Miss X said. 'We got to find the car.'

Miss X later told detectives that Les Murphy got into their vehicle and they all drove to a public telephone box, where he had a conversation with one of his brothers, and she overheard him repeating road directions. Following the phone conversation, they went to Plumpton Road in Blacktown searching for the burnt out car but it wasn't there. The car had disappeared. A resident of the street told them that the night the car was dumped in the street, it was set alight and was then towed away some days later.

Les Murphy then offered to stay with Miss X while others checked a nearby rubbish dump but it was getting late and she had to return to Blacktown Police Station. Miss X refused Murphy's offer, telling him that, while he was wanted and she and those with her were not, 'it would not be all right for them to snoop around' with him.

They dropped Murphy off on a road behind Tich Place, after which Miss X returned to Blacktown Police Station.

To obtain a warrant, Kennedy had to submit a comprehensive document outlining the facts of the case, the reason for requesting a listening device, the names of the persons likely to be recorded on the device and the list of police officers likely to handle the device. Anyone not listed on the document who took part in the operation could render the use of the device 'unlawful' so there was a lot of responsibility involved in ensuring the submission was done correctly. The application was sent to police service lawyers who edited the document for legal jargon and then submitted it to a Supreme Court judge for consideration.

It was about 10pm on Sunday night before the warrant came through. The fact that the case had such a high profile and was at a critical stage led to the warrant being quickly approved. Sergeant Gordon Lever of the Police Departments Legal Services division obtained a Supreme Court warrant after he telephoned Justice John Slattery at his home in Sydney.

Already highly regarded in the legal profession, ironically, Slattery would later investigate the early release of three prisoners from the Broken Hill Correctional Centre in the 1980s, which would contribute to the downfall and eventual imprisonment of corrupt NSW Minister for Corrective Services, Rex 'Buckets' Jackson.

A mini cassette recorder was then taped to the small of Miss X's back and a small microphone was secreted between her breasts to record the conversation. Miss X went back down into the cell and got Travers to repeat on tape what he had previously admitted. 'We made sure we did not tell her what questions to ask but just engage him in conversation, agree to help him if asked and to see what was said,' Ian Kennedy says.

Once again, Travers openly discussed the murder with Miss X. Travers told her to go back to his home in Doonside and get the knife with the 'brown wooden handle out of the kitchen drawer' because that was the one he had used to kill Anita Cobby. Later, he told Miss X they had burned her clothes in an incinerator in the back garden and got rid of the ashes. Their conversation was chilling in its pathology:

Miss X: *John … come close. Why did you have to stop her?*
Travers: *We were all drunk and she fuckin' seen us.*
Miss X: *What, she saw your faces?*
Travers: *Yeah and she got all our names and we just …*
Miss X: *She got your names?*
Travers: *Yeah…*
Miss X: *…And you knew?*
Travers: *Someone had to do it.*
Miss X: *…so what, the others said you had to do it?*
Travers: *…and I said she's gotta be done …*
Miss X: *Who said it had to be done? You?*
Travers: *All of us.*
Miss X: *You all agreed?*
Travers: *Yeah, and then they said, 'Go on Trawney, do your thing' so I just cut her.*
Miss X: *But that's not your thing, John. You haven't done that before, have you?*
Travers: *No*
Miss X: *And she'd seen you. And she saw your teardrop, didn't she?*
Travers: *They weren't going to do it so I had to.*
Miss X: *And the rotten bastards all fucked off on ya.*
Travers: *No one wants to know me now.*
Miss X: *I do John. I still love ya.*

Travers: *Yeah, but I'm just saying they don't and I don't have to stay fucking cool though …*

'I was to get in touch with certain people and tell them to be at Blacktown Police Station between 3.00am and 3.30am and to bring "shotties" [shotguns] in preparation to bust John out,' Miss X told the detectives. Travers had told her this period was the best time for a breakout because there was only a skeleton staff at that time of the morning.

Travers was growing increasingly desperate. 'I've still got that fucking machine gun,' he bluffed, and he implored Miss X to get Gary and Mick Murphy to come with her to court the next day 'with a bit of back up' to blast Travers out. At one point, Miss X proposed plans for breaking out of gaol … crashing a bulldozer through a wall at Blacktown Police Station was one option, derailing the Blacktown train so it would crash into the walls of the police station was another. Travers said he had an oxy acetylene at home, but the cops would see it if they tried to break him out of gaol. Travers said that once he was free, he would escape to New Zealand with his 16-year-old girlfriend Karen. He asked Miss X to give his girlfriend a letter and tell her he was 'sorry from the bottom of me heart'.

When the conversation was over, Miss X returned to the detectives and a technician quickly listened to part of the tape and confirmed the conversation had been recorded successfully. 'Miss X did a great job,' says Kennedy. 'It also shows how much Travers trusted Miss X.'

But still her job wasn't done. Later that same night, another listening devise was fitted to Miss X and she went to talk to Michael Murdoch. Surveillance police knew exactly where he was and that he was at his family home in Mays Hill. There, they had a conversation in a car, with Miss X telling Murdoch that Travers had told her everything that had happened and had given her instructions to tell him what to do with the stolen car.

Murdoch willingly discussed aspects of the murder with her and expressed his amazement that the police knew about their involvement in the murder. Travers had asked her to find the Murphy brothers and tell them to get some guns and come to the police station early in the morning and break him out of gaol. Miss X and Murdoch drove to various addresses looking for Gary and Mick Murphy while, all the while, their conversation was being recorded. Having not been able to find the older

Murphy brothers, she took Murdoch home and drove to the police, who were waiting two or three streets away.

Later that night, police swooped on Michael Murdoch and Les Murphy and arrested them in the early hours of Monday morning. 'There was activity', says Garry Heskett. 'They were starting to arrange passports and so on.' They were not trying to escape the country because of a stolen car, said Kevin Raue, 'so immediately our suspicion was confirmed.'

Police from the Special Weapons and Operations Section (SWOS) stayed with Miss X and her family for most of 1986, until death threats and the looming trial required them to move to a motel under witness protection. Later, Miss X and her family would be given new identities and relocated overseas.

There was no turning back now.

TONY WATERS REMEMBERS

'It was a horrendous case,' says former detective Tony Waters, who was a team leader on the Cobby Case. . 'It was six months out of all our lives that was magnified by the pressures of community expectations, which were enormous. The western suburbs of Sydney were put under the microscope, which was unfortunate but not unexpected given the enormity of the case. The Anita Cobby case had a massive impact on the people who live there. We're coming up for 30 years and people still ask me about it.'

Tony Waters lived in Blacktown from the age of seven. He later went to Lidcombe and Cronulla as a policeman and then went back to Blacktown as a plain clothes detective. 'It was a bit surreal going back to Blacktown where I grew up and knowing a lot of the people I would later lock up …

'There was an avalanche of petty crime growing up in the late 1950s and early 60s. I attended Blacktown West Public School and was going to become a vet so my parents put all their pennies together and sent me off to James Ruse Agricultural High School, a selective high school in the Hills area. That didn't work out, so at age 19 I joined the police.

Blacktown could be rough, he recalls. 'I remember at the age of 14 hopping off the bus at Blacktown Station, having had to catch a couple of buses and trains from Carlingford where I was going to school, and walking past the Robin

Hood Hotel in the main strip. I sat there eating an ice block outside the Maid Marion milk bar in my school uniform and a drunken idiot came out of the Robin Hood Hotel and belted me all over the place for no reason at all. That was typical Blacktown ... smacked around for just being in the wrong place at the wrong time. A rough and ready place ...'

It wasn't all bad, though, as Waters recalls.

'There were lots of good people in Blacktown too, nose to the grindstone types who wanted to do well for their kids, but it seemed as if some of the younger generation coming through in the 1970s didn't want to work as hard. Drugs also became a bigger issue in the district, right out to Richmond. It was a bit of an eye opener for a young detective, even allowing for the fact that I grew up in the area.'

In his role as a detective, Waters often dealt with criminals who were neighbours or friends of his parents. 'Mum and Dad had a lot to do with the Blacktown RSL,' he says, 'and they knew a lot of people. I came home from work one day and they were entertaining friends, and I had just interviewed their son that afternoon about a certain matter. It could be uncomfortable. Mum said their son thought I was a bastard. "Good," I told them. I knew I had done my job then.'

Back in those days, detectives investigated anything from petty theft, assault and armed robbery all the way up to murder. 'It used to peeve me a bit that rank and file police would arrest the bad guys and then hand them over to the detectives and hear no more about it. I thought I would give it a go.'

Waters got 'a tap on the shoulder' to join 'the Ds' when he was stationed at Lidcombe in 1970. 'Our superiors were always keeping an eye on you and seeing how you performed,' he says. In his second year as a 'plain clothes' policeman, he went down to 21 Division for general detective training. He later did a detectives course in 1976. A decade later, he was part of the detectives group based at Blacktown, partnering with Garry Raymond at Blacktown.

'There were more than a dozen detectives at Blacktown on that case so it was a fair crew. Former Blacktown colleagues Kevin Raue and Garry Heskett were at the Homicide Unit in the CIB, and what better men to come back to Blacktown and work on the case,' Waters says. Ian 'Speed' Kennedy came with them to head up the task force.

The Cobby case comprised 'shocking elements', he says. 'It was an unusually violent crime but if you knew John Travers, you'd know why. The Murphy boys were basically petty criminals, with the exception of the eldest brother Mick who had broken out of gaol. I had come across Les Murphy a number of times, not so much his brother Gary, for minor things such as goods in custody etc. I would not have believed Les Murphy would have been involved in something like that, but in my opinion they would not have murdered the girl without John Travers being there. He was the catalyst, but in saying that, all of them agreed to kill her.

'We had lots of leads in the case but once it got to Miss X getting involved, the case opened up in terms of focusing the investigation. Up until then, there was a lot of pressure to break the case and it was difficult because you were chasing so many leads. The stolen car was identified, some of the men were arrested and with Miss X's taped interview on the Sunday, it became a lot easier to track down the people responsible.

We had two family addresses in Granville that we knew the Murphys frequented. Along with Chris O'Toole, Garry Heskett and several others, we went down there late at night to see if they were there. We went to one of the houses and, upon entering, we noticed one of the beds was warm. Les Murphy had just taken off. The only other place we thought he would go to was the other address so we went down there and fortunately that's where he was, lying on the floor between two women on a mattress with a blanket over them'

How ironic, Waters thought. Having women hide him after what he had done to Anita Cobby.

'I was involved in the interviewing of Les Murphy and I also did the run-around of the crime scene with his brother Gary. After his arrest, Les was compliant and was resolved to his situation. He was happy to get it all of his chest. As far as blame went, they all pointed in different directions and nominated John Travers as the killer.

'[Les Murphy] was shocked by the demonstrations at Blacktown Court, as they all were … that really freaked him out. It was fairly frightening to drive through a group of people who were roaring with abuse, banging on the car roof and to get past them.' The fact that Murphy and the others were scared to death wasn't lost on the detectives. Weeks before, they had driven Anita Cobby to her death without a concern in the world.

'Ordinary people were aghast. I was amazed at the fellows working on the Westpoint site who joined in the abuse and dropped rope nooses from the roof.'

Once the men responsible were in custody 'it was as if the pressure valve was released ... it made you feel like a hero. There were no winners in a case like this, however, just the satisfaction.'

When he gave evidence about the arrest of Les Murphy, Waters had to memorise eleven pages of evidence – verbatim. 'It was extremely difficult, but you had to put the time and effort into getting it right because we needed to ensure the conviction was warranted.' Today, Waters doesn't think too much about the men who murdered Anita Cobby. 'I like to think they spend a lot of time at night looking over their shoulder.'

In March 1993, Waters left the force and took on the management of a service station/car wash/convenience store operation. 'I remember saying to my wife if I ever want to go back to the police, just shoot me. Within 17 months, I re-joined the police because I was only marking time. Although the business was a million dollar operation, I ended up going back and becoming the Detective Chief Inspector at Campbelltown from 1998 to 2006.'

Waters was with the NSW Police Force for 36 years when he had a bad reaction to medication that triggered PTSD. 'I was a Senior Crime Manager at the time and had seen police respond differently to situations and I thought a lot of these PTSD issues were overstated,' he says. '[But] things I had pushed under over the years rose to the surface again, and the Anita Cobby case was certainly part of that. Getting startled at night in bed and sitting bolt upright – and the odd nightmare – it's taken a long time to come out the other side.'

Police now recognise that there are many problems associated with the job that can lay dormant for years but then resurface. 'The only psychology sessions you had in the early days were a couple of beers with the boys at the pub, but they now recognise that PTSD as a very significant condition,' says Waters.

'The process is still on-going ... counselling sessions help, but I must admit the odd beer with old mates and having a chat about the old days helps just as much. The Blacktown guys are central to that...'

CHAPTER SIX

The Arrest

Kennedy: We have been told that you and John Travers, and Gary, Les and Mick Murphy grabbed her in the car and took her to Reen Road where you all raped her and cut her throat.
Murdoch: I never fucked her. Travers cut her throat. I ran away.
Kennedy: Where is the car now?
Murdoch: I don't know.
Kennedy: You told us earlier that you had nothing to do with her murder, but that isn't correct?
Murdoch: Yeah, but honest, I didn't fuck her.
Official police transcript, 24 February 1986

Shortly after midnight on 24 February, Detective Sergeant Roger Kilburn of the Technical Survey Unit of the Bureau of Criminal Intelligence met Detective Sergeant Ian Kennedy at an address in Booth Street, Westmead, and arrested Michael Murdoch. On the way to Blacktown Police Station, the 18-year-old admitted for the first time being with Travers and the Murphy brothers from the time Mrs Cobby was abducted in Newton Road to her death at Prospect. There was no particular reason Cobby was targeted, Murdoch said, except that she was there.

'Yeah, it did happen,' he told the Detectives, 'but I didn't touch her.'

Asked by Kennedy for his version of events on the night Anita Cobby was killed, Murdoch was careful to minimise his level of participation.

'Well, I was sitting at John's place and they came around John's place. They been out drinking and they said, "Let's go for a drive" and I went with them … (We) drove around Blacktown and we seen her and they said, "Let's pick her up" and I said, "No" but they went ahead and did it. They took her up to Prospect, took her to the paddock and raped her and then cut her throat. Then we went home.'

Murdoch was careful enough not to use too many personal pronouns – 'they said', 'they went' and 'they took her' – but he admitted that all of them had discussed the fact that Anita Cobby had heard their names and seen their faces, so it was decided to kill her. Travers, Murdoch said, was the only one 'game enough to do it'.

According to Murdoch, it was Travers who dragged a screaming Anita Cobby into the car and then punched her in the mouth to silence her. Michael Murphy was also holding her, with his hand over her mouth. Once she was inside the car, they ripped her clothes from her body and Travers and Mick Murphy raped her in the back seat.

When the car stopped at a garage on the Great Western Highway opposite the Prospect Hotel, Les Murphy paid for the petrol with a $20 note taken from Cobby's purse. It was Travers' idea to go to the paddock at the end of Reen Road to rape her. Once there, Murdoch said, Gary and Les Murphy raped Anita Cobby beside the fence, then he jumped over the fence and, in his own words, 'helped' her through the barbed wire and into the paddock.

In a second interview, however, Murdoch admitted to Ian Kennedy that it was he who the witness on Newton Road saw help Travers pull the woman into the car. As the car approached the petrol station, Murdoch punched her 'to shut her up'. He even conceded that he too had dragged Anita Cobby through the barbed wire, rather than 'helping' her through as he had suggested in the first interview, and he had attempted to rape her but was 'unsuccessful,' meaning her couldn't get an erection.

Les Murphy kicked her, Murdoch said, and Mrs Cobby was raped repeatedly in the paddock. Afterwards, Travers said, 'I'm gonna cut her throat, she's recognised the whole lot of us.' Murdoch said that he walked off at this point after seeing Travers sitting on Mrs Cobby's back with her hair pulled back. When Travers joined the others back in the car, he had 'blood all over his hands and on his clothing.'

Back at Travers' Doonside home later that night, Anita Cobby's clothes and bag were burnt – everything except for her shoes. According to Murdoch, Gary Murphy asked if he could have them. Mick and Gary Murphy drove off in the stolen car, Les Murphy went into the caravan with Lisa Travers at the back of the home and Travers and Murdoch tried to get some sleep inside the house.

After police interviewed Murdoch, Graham Rosetta went to the cells and woke John Travers. 'I have further information in relation to the

Cobby case which indicates you were involved,' Rosetta began.

'Who gave us up?' Travers demanded as he jumped to his feet. 'What about the others, have you got them too …?'

Rosetta asked who Travers was referring to.

'The Murphys,' Travers volunteered, 'Les, Gary and Mick, and Mick, Mick Murdoch.'

'Were they all involved?' Rosetta asked. Travers said yes.

'Who killed her,' Rosetta asked.

'I did,' he admitted.

Travers told Rosetta and Detective Senior Constable Paul Rynne that he, Michael Murdoch and all three Murphy brothers were involved in the crime. In a signed record of interview, Travers said that when he saw Anita Cobby walking on Newton Road, he told the others to stop the car.

'We were just going to rape her,' he told the detectives. With the help of Murdoch, he dragged Anita Cobby into the car. She was raped in the back seat, bashed and robbed, and then after they bought petrol, they took her to the paddock on Reen Road. 'When we were finished, we were worried that she'd identify us, so um, we agreed to get rid of her,' Travers said. 'She was laying there unconscious and I went up and cut her throat.'

'They were saying "what will we do if she identifies us" and then I heard "Trawney, do your thing."'

Asked what he thought that meant, Travers replied, 'I thought they meant get rid of her, cut her throat.' He crouched over her, pulled her head back by the hair and cut her throat. He conceded that he 'pressed a fair bit, the knife's pretty sharp.'

Back home, Travers washed the blood off his clothes in the shower while Murdoch and the Murphys burnt Cobby's belongings in the backyard. The ashes were later taken to a local tip with a load of rubbish.

Five days after the murder, the stolen car was dumped in Plumpton Road and burnt out. Travers said that Gary Murphy and he had borrowed a car from a friend, taken the stolen car to an isolated road and poured petrol on it. Travers and the others knew police were looking for the Holden in relation to the Cobby murder so he personally lit the fire.

That night, police raided Travers' home in Doonside looking for Les Murphy. He wasn't there but Lisa Travers, Murphy's teenage partner at the time, was taken from the caravan at the back of the house and interviewed at Blacktown Police Station. She didn't know where Les was, she told the police, but they already knew of a number of known addresses where he and his brothers could be hiding.

At 2.30am the following morning, Les Murphy was arrested at his sister's house in Railway Parade, Granville. Detective Constable Garry Heskett remembers, 'When we captured Les Murphy, there were two houses where he could be hiding and we had them both covered. I walked into the bedroom of the first house, which was only a mattress on the floor, and it was still warm. Where was he?

'He'd run out the back of that house up to the house where the other team was waiting. We went up there, got everyone out of bed and put them in the lounge room. Detective Tony Waters rustled two women who were sleeping in the front room because we wanted everyone in the lounge room. He yelled out, "Gaz get in here" and Les was lying in between the two women with a sheet over him.'

Detective Constable Paul Davies told Les Murphy he was under arrest for the murder of Anita Cobby. In transferring Murphy to Blacktown Police Station, the defendant was questioned in the car. 'Yes, I was there,' Murphy told the detectives, 'but Travers did it, not me.'

Waters: What do you mean 'Travers did it'?

Murphy: He cut her throat. The rest of them just rooted her.

Waters: Why did Travers cut her throat?

Murphy: Well, we talked about it and we all agreed that she could have recognised us.

Waters: Who's we?

Murphy: My brothers, Mick and Gary, Mick Murdoch and Travers.

Waters: Did you have sex with the girl?

Les Murphy tried, he said, but 'couldn't'. His brother Mick 'wouldn't let me.'

The Anita Cobby task force had arrested three of the main offenders and had the other two men responsible in their sights. 'At about 4am, I went to Mr and Mrs Lynch's house,' Ian Kennedy remembers, 'and informed them of the arrests. What was good news for them was also extremely heartbreaking as I had to tell them there were two more men involved – a total of five, in all – and that Anita had been repeatedly sexually assaulted for a number of hours before being brutality murdered.

I wanted them to hear it from the police rather than from the media, who we knew would soon descend on the house after the arrests were reported.'

'The press knew we had arrested someone and were bound to release the news soon. I had to be truthful because I didn't want them to hear about the other suspects from the media. If Grace and Garry had said, "We've heard from the press that you're looking for two more, why didn't you tell us?" I wouldn't have been able to face them.'

From 4.15am to 8.30am that morning, Detectives Kevin Raue and Garry Heskett interviewed 'a very compliant' Les Murphy. 'He admitted to everything,' says Heskett, 'although there was absolutely no remorse.'

John Travers, Michael Murdoch and his two brothers were with him in the stolen car, Les Murphy told the detectives, when they abducted Anita Cobby off the street. 'We took her up a dead end road near the drive-in at Blacktown. They pulled her gear off, and we just took her down into the paddock.'

Les Murphy admitted that he punched Anita once at the paddock and walked her down to the clearing but he did not have sex with her. Travers, Gary and Mick Murphy all attempted to have sex with her but 'ran away when interrupted by a car that drove down the road.' When they returned, Mrs Cobby was still unconscious, he said. He had wanted to 'have sex with her ordinary' but his brother Mick wouldn't let him.

'Travers cut her throat with his knife,' Les Murphy confirmed. 'We went back to my place where we burnt her clothes in the backyard.'

At dawn, Michael Murdoch was taken from the cells at Blacktown for a 'run-around' of the crime scene. Says Kennedy, 'This is where the offender (if he agrees) is taken back to the scene of the crime and other critical locations where he can detail the incident and indicate any land features associated with the crime.' Photos were taken so that the jury could later see where the incident took place.

Kennedy and Detective Hugh Dundas took Murdoch to Newton Road, where he indicated the spot where Anita had been abducted, then to Reen Road, at the point where she was dragged through the barbed wire fence and then to the spot where she was raped and murdered. At the same time, Graham Rosetta, Kevin Raue and Garry Heskett took Les Murphy to his Doonside address where he indicated where they had burned Anita's belongings. Showing Raue a concrete slab in the backyard, Murphy said, 'The fire was there. All the ashes went to the tip … '

When asked who was at the fire, he said, 'All of us.' Mick Murphy, he said, had lit the fire with petrol.

On Monday, 24 February, the three suspects were formally interviewed. This was before electronic interviews, which are used today, and the police had to hand write and then type out all the questions and any of the answers given by the offenders. All three men made certain admissions about the murder, each blaming the others while seeking to minimise their own roles in the crime.

Piecing together the events of that night, the scenario unfolded pretty much as the detectives had suspected. The three men had stolen a car and together with Les Murphy's brothers, Mick and Gary, they had all been drinking in Doonside at a local hotel. Needing money for petrol, the idea of a bag-snatch in Blacktown quickly escalated into a deliberate plan to 'grab a girl and rape her' and later, her murder. They saw Anita Cobby walking westward down Newton Road heading towards the Walters Road intersection shortly before 10pm.

'Someone in the car suggested they grab her and have some fun,' Michael Murdoch said. Forced into the car, she was stripped naked at knife point and sexually assaulted by Travers and Mick Murphy in the back seat while Murdoch drove.

Stealing money from her purse, some of the men purchased petrol from a 24-hr service station on the Great Western Highway, while two others sat on top of her and held the knife to her face so she wouldn't scream. They then decided to take her to Reen Road, where she was dragged through the barbed wire fence and the men took turns raping her. During the assault, a car drove along the road and shone a light across the paddock. It was teenager Paul McGaughey and his girlfriend, looking for any sign of the missing girl. The five men hid in the long grass until the car left.

When they were finished with her, it was decided that because she had seen their faces and heard their names, Anita Cobby had to be killed because she could identify them later. Mick Murphy had goaded Travers to 'do your thing,' which they all knew was cutting her throat with a large hunting knife. After Travers came back covered in blood, they took her clothes and bag and drove back to Travers' house in Doonside and disposed of them.

After interviewing Travers, Murdoch and Les Murphy, they were each charged with abduction, robbery, rape and murder and related offences. The police involved in the arrest of Murdoch and Les Murdoch had worked through the night, but their job wasn't yet over.

There were two more to be found.

CHAPTER SEVEN

The Boys

On 16 April 1986, Detectives Graham Rosetta, Paul Davies and Phillip Gaspert went to Parklea Gaol to question 19-year-old John Raymond Travers. After acknowledging that he had admitted killing Anita Cobby, Travers was asked about the knife he used. It was a Montana brand knife with a wooden handle and a blade about 20cm long, Travers told them, and cost about $30. He purchased the knife from the Ben Bow Archery Shop in Macquarie Street, Parramatta. The detectives showed Travers a similar knife they had purchased at the shop, but Travers said the blade looked 'a bit shorter.'

When they asked Travers where the murder weapon was now, he said the last time he saw the knife, it was in the kitchen draw at his Doonside home. Couldn't they find it?

It's sobering to remember that John Travers was still only 18 when he abducted, assaulted, raped, robbed and murdered Anita Cobby. His friend Michael Murdoch, who was part of the gang of five, was six months younger than Travers. While most young men that age are usually enjoying their first year out of high school – working their first job, serving an apprenticeship or even starting a higher education course – Murdoch was 'adrift … completely lost'. Travers was a budding psychopath ready to explode on society.

Born on 27 February 1967, John Travers had grown up with a horrendous home life. His father Ken was a violent alcoholic and his mother, Sharon, was an obese invalid trapped in her own home by her weight and bouts of depression. She gave birth to son John at the age of 15 and went on to have another six children. The family lived on social security handouts, with Sharon and Ken unable or unwilling to care for their children or maintain a home and provide for them.

John Travers was sexually abused by a relative, and in the words of one of his lawyers, grew up 'isolated and vilified' by the world. Exposed to violence from an early age, his father would choke him until he fell unconscious. Later, as a wild teenager, he physically fought with his father. Travers later told psychiatrists that abusing alcohol and drugs for him were 'a means of escape' after his mother told him that his father often wanted to kill him. At age 14, Travers would drink a bottle of whiskey in one session and was a frequent marijuana user. He was also beginning to experiment with harder drugs.

The Travers family moved to Tich Place, Doonside, in the late 1970s after repeated complaints about their squalid existence and behaviour at Mt Druitt. Neighbours had complained about 'harassment and intimidation' when Travers was not even a teenager. The Travers family were given an unremarkable white weatherboard bungalow, similar to thousands of housing commission dwellings that sprawled westward from the edge of Blacktown. The house had to be modified to help the youngest child, who suffered from spina bifida.

In 1983, Ken Travers left the family home but the domestic situation had already deteriorated. An often bed-ridden Sharon Travers could neither control her children nor care for them. The younger Travers children were often sent to foster homes when their mother was hospitalised. John was close to his grandmother and moved in with her at Wentworthville for about a year, but her death from cancer had a devastating effect on him.

Sharon Travers suffered from Cushing's disease which is caused by excess growth of the pituitary gland at the base of the brain. The pituitary gland releases cortisol, a stress hormone, which also controls the body's use of carbohydrates, fats and proteins, and a by-product of Cushing's disease is gross obesity. Sometimes weighing up to 130 kilograms, Sharon Travers required frequent hospital visits and home help. District nurses refused to visit the household because of the squalid conditions and the fact that they were intimidated by the other members of the family.

With their father gone and their mother bedridden, John and his sister Lisa looked after the family. John tried to be the disciplinarian, but just as he had been bashed by his father for no particular reason, he too flogged his younger brothers when he thought they needed it. It was all he knew.

Travers stole from neighbours, shot birds with a .22 calibre rifle from the back porch of his home and cooked them, took livestock from nearby farms and slaughtered them primarily to feed the family, but also because it was fun. Psychologists' reports also stated that he was interested in witchcraft, that he was cruel to animals and that he also had sex with them. Long before the murder, Travers had earned 'a reputation for cruelty and perversity which made some people nervous, if not scared.'

According to psychologist Dr Geoffrey Fox, Travers developed a 'distorted idea of morality' growing up in the family home. The psychologist reported that Travers' father would encourage him to bring home young girls and have sex with them under the floorboards of their modest Doonside home while he watched.

Psychologist Allan Perry stated if 'the familial environment doesn't provide a socialising atmosphere, a normal personality won't develop.' John Travers was anything but normal.

Travers kept two pet bull terriers, one called 'Arse' and the other 'Slut'. No one else was allowed to interact with the animals because he wanted them only to answer to his command. On one occasion, he fed the dogs a live chicken to 'give them the taste of blood'. A relative of the family later alleged that Travers had sex with his dogs to keep them 'faithful'.

Nicknamed 'Trawney' by his friends, Travers had convictions for possessing marijuana, illegally using a motor vehicle, two counts of car thief, possessing house-breaking implements, receiving stolen goods and possessing a shortened firearm. In trouble with the law from the age of ten, he spent a year at Cobham Remand Centre, a juvenile detention centre at Werrington, after being committed by his mother, who reasoned that her son's problems were caused by 'being around the wrong people'.

Travers left school before gaining any certification. Asked to leave Shalvey High School for 'mucking up', he was expelled from Doonside High for exposing his penis to a teacher. In 1982, when he lived with his grandmother, he enrolled in Newman Catholic High School at Greystanes in Year 10, but dropped out. He worked for a short time at Riverstone abattoirs, which skilled him in the use of a knife, but Travers preferred to collect the dole and live off the proceeds of crime.

Towards the end of his school years, Travers started giving himself homemade tattoos by wrapping a needle with cotton, dipping it in Indian ink and then pricking his skin. By the time he was 18, he had a gallery of ink images over his body, including many on his penis … initials, hearts, a pair of lips and the words 'I like fucking cunts'. The most distinctive tattoo, however, was a single teardrop under his left eye. Whatever the significance of the mark, it made him very recognisable, especially to those he attacked.

In the six months month before the Anita Cobby murder, detectives later discovered, Travers raped at least four other people – a teenage girl he assaulted in Toongabbie, a suburb east of Blacktown in August 1985; a woman in Port Lincoln, South Australia, on his way to Western Australia with a group of mates; a young man the group met in Mandurah, south of Perth and another girl he met at a party with Les Murphy in January 1986.

After the attack on the young girl in Toongabbie, Travers and his friends drove across the desert in a utility truck, buying drugs and stealing goods to pay their way west. After the rape of the woman in Port Lincoln, Travers panicked, realising the girl knew too much about the group and had seen the tattooed teardrop. The group returned to Sydney, leaving the Ute in Adelaide. Incredibly, Travers was able to convince his uncle to drive him back to Port Lincoln so the group could pick up their vehicle and continue their trip to Western Australia.

Arriving in the coast town of Mandurah and looking for drugs, they met up with another group of youths including an openly gay 17-year-old male. The young man agreed to pose for some pornographic photos that Travers said he would sell back in Sydney and share the profits with him. Travers, 'high on alcohol and drugs', then violently bashed and raped the young man as his friends looked on and took photos with an Instamatic Polaroid camera.

During the brutal rape, Travers reportedly put a knife to the young man's throat and said, 'Buck, you bastard, or I'll cut your throat.' It was eerily similar to the attack on Anita Cobby – police later suspected that he was anally raping her when he pulled her hair back and cut her throat. After the rape, the young man collapsed to the floor in agony and Travers kicked him in the ribs, warning him to 'keep his mouth shut or he would come back and kill him.'

The teenager was taken to the local police station by a youth worker to make a complaint against a Sydney man known as 'Trawney' Travers. Police later interviewed two of Travers' friends, but not Travers, and charged them with assault, theft and using a false name, adding that they should 'tell your friend to get an AIDS test.' The group left Western Australia soon after. The young man was so shaken by the attack that he later declined to cooperate with police and refused to lay charges.

It was clear Travers didn't view sexuality in a normal way. Says Garry Raymond, 'Instead of interaction and attachment, for Travers it was a demonstration of power, a situation to exploit and something to use to degrade others, male or female.' Travers' sexual drive was personal gratification. He couldn't care about the object – animal, boy, girl, woman, man.

'It was a hero and follower relationship with Travers and Murdoch. Travers was a mentor, but there was no psychological hold over Murdoch. He was a willing participant and could have left the relationship at any time. Travers didn't have the ability to have relationships … because of his narcissism, he wouldn't have regarded Murdoch as anything more than a 'hanger-onner'. They were found together in bed so there may have been a sexual dimension their relationship.'

Back in Sydney, Travers showed his uncle's defacto wife the pictures taken of the rape on the teenaged boy in Western Australia. Travers trusted his 'aunt' and told her of his many attacks, including the girl he assaulted in Port Lincoln, in an attempt to impress her. His friends had gang raped the girl and had done 'horrid things to her', he said.

Travers actually enjoyed the notoriety of being a rapist among his social group. He didn't view himself as bisexual or even homosexual, but told friends that when presented with the opportunity, 'You've got to try it.' Travers hated homosexual men, he told his aunt. He would go out and bash them, then rape them for good measure.

Travers' 'aunt' anonymously contacted local police about the attacks but Travers went underground and was able to hide from them. That was, until February 1986.

Mick Murdoch idolised John Travers. Born on 1 September 1967, Murdoch first came into Travers' orbit when they lived three doors from each other in Mt Druitt in the late 1970s. Soon, the pair was inseparable, despite the best efforts of Murdoch's mother Rose. The eldest of six children in a single-parent household, Mick frightened his mother who was afraid of Travers' influence over her son. When she found her son smoking marijuana with Travers at age 13, she rang Sharon Travers and told her that she was going to call the police. This call resulted in the pair's first conviction.

A friend of the pair later remarked, 'No matter what John did, Mick did the same thing. They spoke the same, they swore the same, they dressed the same, their haircuts were the same. When John shaved his head, Mick Murdoch did the same. It was just like two peas in a pod. When John did something violent, Mick'd just stand there and let John do it and wouldn't attempt to stop him in any way.'

Like Sharon Travers, Murdoch's mother also suffered health problems. A chain smoker with only one lung, Murdoch's mother would die tragically from emphysema in 1989. Mrs Murdoch at least tried to remove her son from Travers' influence and provide a home for her large family. The Murdochs moved to Mays Hill, a suburb near Parramatta, but Travers and Murdoch remained 'thick as thieves'... wagging school together and hanging around local pool rooms, doing drugs and drinking, stealing cars and breaking into houses. They tattooed each other, body-pierced each other and even shared the same girls. The pair had a number of heterosexual, teenaged partners and they had no problems forcing themselves on girls or bashing them into having sex if they wanted them to.

They were almost like twins physically, but psychologically, they were the opposite sides of the same bad coin – Travers, outward going and egocentric, Murdoch, the quiet one, but cold. Travers was the leader and Murdoch the follower. They were blood brothers, each cutting their hands and mixing the blood to complete the initiation.

At Travers' 18th birthday, Travers brought a lamb along, had sex with it and then cut its throat. Gary and Michael Murphy were also present that night and saw Travers lying beside the dead lamb, then plunging a knife into its belly. He then cooked it on an open fire, ate it and threw the bones into a neighbour's swimming pool. Travers was 'stoned off his tits' and had drunk a bottle of whisky, his mother later said. The following morning, there wasn't a fence between the Doonside home and the next-door neighbours. Travers had torn all the palings off to fuel the fire to roast the lamb.

Like the Murphy brothers, Mick Murdoch did nothing but smile and laugh at John Travers' craziness.

John was his hero.

John Raymond Travers once remarked, 'If I'm ever going to go to gaol, it'll be for something big.'

GRAHAM ROSETTA REMEMBERS

Graham Rosetta started as a police cadet in 1964 before becoming a constable the following year. He served in the force for 25 years, but makes no hesitation in saying today: 'I never came across anything like the brutality of the people involved in the Anita Cobby case.'

'I was in Blacktown for two and a half years,' Rosetta remembers. 'Before that, I was in the CIB Breaking Squad in the city. The area was made up of typical Western Sydney working class people, no airs and graces needed, and that's not "westie" bashing because I lived in the west. In Western Sydney, 16 to 25-year-olds were highly represented in crime figures, but it must be said that a lot of injury and disadvantage was self-inflicted. Some people there made many poor choices.

'26 Division (Blacktown and Mt Druitt) investigated drugs, domestic violence, theft, crimes of dishonesty, property offenses. I worked with Detective Paul Rynne, who was my full-time partner at Blacktown at the time.

Rosetta says he became very close with his colleagues who, like fellow survivors of a major catastrophe, can understand each other in a way few others can. 'There is a bond between the detectives involved in a murder investigation. You have to understand everyone is professional, some get on better than others, that's just a fact of life. Any working team forms a bond because you become close investigating a case.

'We didn't have any pressure from senior officers to "get this thing solved". Everyone worked hard toward a common goal. As far as teamwork was concerned, the effect is incredible and that's only to be expected. Most cops are good people, in many ways were even more offended with what happens in the world – we are citizens after all – and then we have to go out and investigate it.'

The real fear, says Rosetta, was that these offenders would offend again.

'There was common purpose in the group, and for Murdoch to have the audacity to say he was asleep in the back with three blokes raping a woman defies belief. It was just cold blooded lust ... an attitude that "we can do anything we want".

'The reporting of an abduction in Blacktown was the start of it all, that there was a number of men involved. From there, we chipped away at the case to find the men responsible. The eyewitnesses on Newton Road were very important, not in the actual identification of the people responsible, but we were able to put together a very clear picture of what happened ... a lovely, clean-living young woman, going about her life after knocking off work, walking home at night and abducted off the street by these animals.'

People wanted to help them. 'We had a lot of leads, some false ones too, but that goes with the territory. We were able to say it was not a domestic situation and that cut out a lot of other avenues we were bound to look at. Domestic relationships cause the vast majority of murders so if you can eliminate those early on, you can save all the inherent heavy legwork involved ... weeks and months of investigation.

'The information that we gathered about John Travers was that he and Murdoch had been involved in the rape of a teenage boy in WA, and a knife had been produced. That was well-documented but the victim declined to press charges because he was afraid. It was important we knew the type of person we were dealing with.

'Travers had also cut the throat of a sheep in his backyard not long before, so things were pretty much pointing in his direction. I had not come across any of the men in my role as a detective in Blacktown. I had come across Mick Murphy years before, but the other men were only teenagers and in their early 20s.

'The fact was at the time Miss X emerged, the main three suspects were in custody. Certainly her evidence later on in court was very important; [she was] very brave, make no mistake about that, so we can never minimise the gravity of her evidence.

'Among the protestors and demonstrations at Blacktown, there were a lot of faces in the crowd I'd seen on the other side of the fence. It's funny because people have various reasons for doing what they do. Sometimes I wonder, were some people perhaps trying to cleanse their own souls by getting on the right side of law and order?'

The fact that some people harboured the wanted criminals still amazes Rosetta.

'Unfortunately you are always going to have people who protect criminals no matter what they've done. The arrest of the Murphy brothers was not a difficult operation ... in many ways, it was completely by the book. There was no real drama with the arrest of any of them. Travers and Murdoch were at the home of a relative, Les Murphy was at home and the other Murphys were being hidden by two women.

'In saying that, they were killers, and we were cognisant of the potential that they could be armed. They were violent men and we didn't take them lightly.'

Each of the culprits made certain admissions during official interviews, but all except Travers tried to minimise his own involvement in the crime. 'As far as I'm concerned, it just confirmed they were gutless and not prepared to take responsibility for their crimes, nor were they prepared to show any remorse for their actions.'

The most damning thing about the case was the attitude of the men, Rosetta says. '"We'll go out and steal a car, then we'll just drive down the road and abduct any woman we want off the street and rape her." Whether they end up killing her or not, the deed has already been set in motion. That's the evil of the whole thing. It wasn't a spur of the moment decision. It never was'.

'It was a lack of respect for people in my view; the lack of respect that had been engendered in them is pretty frightening. It's the erosion of respect in the community ... for police, teachers, doctors, nurses and ambos ... authority in general, but also of their fellow citizens.

'Don't forget, at the trial, not one of the five men ever said sorry or showed remorse of any kind. Their behaviour during court was despicable. For all of John Travers' faults, he at least pleaded guilty and he never appealed. He was the only one of the five who admitted having intercourse with her ... as far as the others were concerned, they minimised their involvement, blaming each other.'

Rosetta makes another observation. 'The other interesting thing is, society today has a massive problem with drugs, ice in particular, yet none of them put up the excuse they were under the influence of drugs or alcohol. We're too happy today to say, "Oh well he was on drugs and he didn't know what he was doing." How often do defence lawyers put that up? It makes your blood boil.'

At the trial, Travers pleaded guilty, but it didn't make the job any easier. 'In hindsight, having the main offender plead guilty may have made our case stronger but the jury weren't to know that. Juries are funny cattle and I've seen some acquittals in very strong cases, so I'm always extremely worried when the foreman comes back in to deliver he verdict.

'In the Janine Balding case in 1988, it was right in our backyard, as far as murders go, and that case was just as bad as the Cobby case. The age of the people involved was immaterial. They knew that it was wrong and showed a total disregard for human life and liberty. It was history repeating itself in so many respects and the yet the criminals were younger, which made it even more wrong.'

Though Rosetta doesn't count Anita's case as a victory, he was at least pleased with the sentences her killers received.

'If you take a life, you get life. How many convictions for murder have we had and there hasn't been that many life sentences, have there? If this wasn't a case for "life behind bars" then nothing was. My personal belief is "life means life" but there are still some people who see merit in the death penalty. The Yanks have varying degrees of murder up to the fourth degree. I never agreed with [the death penalty], but I'm starting to think maybe there is some merit in it. In cases of first-degree murder, they get life.'

Murder is murder, any way you look at it, Rosetta says. 'Some unfortunate life has been taken and in lots of cases, there are unfortunate women who have met the same fate, although not in the same circumstances as this case.

'I have no doubt there are people out there now who, given the opportunity to release [Anita's killers] would consider it, despite the fact that their papers are marked "never to be released". It wouldn't take much ... a government with reform agendas and revisionist agendas, and it could happen. I fear that it might. That will only happen if we forget what happened to Anita.'

'Anyone who thinks they can rehabilitate John Travers has rocks in their head. He's an evil man; some people are just born that way, that's all there is to it. It was always my belief that because Travers had this knife with him on the night that they were prepared to go that one step further ... I don't believe it was just the fear of being identified.

'Just as many people in society refuse to accept that fact ... the poor bugger had a difficult upbringing. Lots of people have that start in life. Plenty of good citizens had a rough upbringing and they don't go down the path [Travers] did.

Michael Murdoch was the same. Travers was the prime mover and certainly the most violent of the group; he was the youngest at age 19 but also the leader. He had an incredible influence on Murdoch. The three Murphy brothers were bloody hopeless career criminals ... they didn't have a brain of their own to think with, and that's not being unkind to them.'

Rosetta identifies with Anita Cobby not just as a victim, but also as a young woman with her whole future ahead of her. 'I have daughters too,' he says, 'and as I got older and my own children grew up, I couldn't help but draw parallels with my own children. I would like to think that my respect for Anita and my understanding of her situation allowed me to get to know the type of person she was.'

The Lynches were wonderful people, Rosetta remembers, 'stoic and faith-filled ... I have nothing but admiration for them. The strength they showed was incredible, everyone who knew them had exactly the same opinion. God knows what personal horrors they went though. The death of your own child is something you never get over, and in circumstances like that, I honestly don't know how they did it.

Having met her parents, her sister and friends, Anita was obviously a lovely young woman, Rosetta maintains. 'I'm talking character-wise, not just physical beauty, but as a person. You can't just pay her any bigger compliment than that.'

CHAPTER EIGHT

The Search

On Friday, 21 February, local resident Anne King had her car stolen and reported it lost at Blacktown Police Station. A close confident of the Cobby family she, like the rest of the community, was still reeling from the as yet unsolved murder of Anita Cobby. Three days later, Mrs King was contacted by police to come to the station … her car had been found. She was inside the station when the three men were arrested and charged with the murder.

'Standing in front of me were the men responsible for the murder of someone special to me and my family,' she later wrote.

Just three weeks into the investigation, hundreds of thousands of people thought Anita was someone special.

When the Sydney media learned of the arrests of three local men on 24 February, 1986 for the murder of Anita Cobby, they swarmed all over Blacktown Police Station. The public, hearing of the arrests on the news, gathered outside Blacktown Police Station which was positioned next to the local court house where the men would be appearing at 10am to be charged with the crime. By the time the detectives brought the defenders to court, there were at least three hundred people on the footpaths outside the courthouse – mainly women, but also men, grandparents and children – spilling over onto the road and stopping traffic. Some were holding placards, others were yelling obscenities. Workers on top of Westpoint Plaza across the road hung a noose from the roof of the building.

'It was quite scary for us,' says Ian Kennedy, who was in a squad car with Mick Murdoch coming back from the crime scene run-around, 'and we were the good guys.

'It could very easily have gone south if one of us had overreacted. If one of the crooks had lashed out at members of the public, it could have got extremely bad. No doubt at all that the demonstration rattled them ...

there was fear in their eyes and their heads were down. They just wanted to get out of there.'

Detective Tony Waters was in the other car guarding Les Murphy. 'It was a strange scene,' he recalls. 'There was a lot of screaming and placards being waved and, of course, someone put up a noose. People were thumping the car … the car window was half open and someone reached in to punch Les, I guess, but they missed and it grazed me.' 'Show your face, screamed one woman as Murdoch attempted to hide his face underneath his sloppy joe,' one journalist reported. 'Kill the bastard,' yelled another, as the crowd stepped forward and surrounded the police car. The crew on top of Westpoint started chanting 'hang the bastards, hang the bastards.' One Blacktown resident was quoted saying, 'Not even animals would kill like that.' Some of the posters read, 'WRAN re-think the parole system,' 'Gaol them for the rest of their natural life' and 'Casterate (sic) the animals.'

Inside the court, those in the small gallery area were warned by local magistrate Neil McDermid that no outburst would be tolerated. Appearing before the court were:

John Raymond Travers, 19, unemployed, Jewelsford Road, Wentworthville
Michael James Murdoch, 18, unemployed, Booth Street, Mays Hill
Leslie Murphy, 22, maintenance worker, Tich Place, Doonside

Travers, who joined the pair via a passageway from the adjacent cells, was wearing a blue checked shirt, blue jeans and sneakers. Murphy, in bare feet wearing a checked flannel shirt and blue jeans, looked at the floor as the charges were read out. Murdoch, wearing a light blue sloppy joe and blue jeans, was also shoeless.

Public solicitor Craig Patrick represented the three men. The police prosecutor was Bruce Newling. No details of the alleged crimes were given but the three men were charged with 'murdering, assaulting, abducting and robbing' Anita Cobby at Prospect on 2 February. Murphy was also charged with receiving four wheels and two seat covers valued at $1000 belonging to Bruce Commins of Seven Hills. Travers was also charged with two counts of assaulting another woman at Toongabbie on 8 January.

The hearing lasted only five minutes and none of the accused spoke. All three were remanded into custody while detectives continued their enquiries to locate brothers Mick and Gary Murphy, who were now implicated in the crime. The media ran hard with the story, showing mug shots of both men on the front pages of both Sydney newspapers. That five local men, including three brothers from the same family, one of them an escaped prisoner, were involved in the murder of an innocent woman generated a lot of media attention and public outrage.

NSW Premier Neville Wran appealed for calm, 'While everyone can understand why people are disgusted and angry about the case, the public interest would be served by remaining calm.' Blacktown MP John Aquilina, the newly appointed Minister for Natural Resources, stated that the State Government had indicated its concern about the case by doubling the reward to $100,000 for information about the killers of Anita Cobby

The issue of law and order was raging in the community. In the six months before the murder, 75 prisoners had escaped for NSW gaols. Although most had been recaptured, nine of the top ten most wanted criminals in the state were gaol escapees. The bigger question was how did someone with such an extensive criminal record like Mick Murphy work the system to obtain a low security clearance and then basically walk out of gaol? A subsequent inquiry revealed a lapse in the prisoner classification procedures.

'We believed we were on the right track but needed more, so we hit the press again and another public appeal was broadcast asking for help,' says Ian Kennedy. Police learned that on the night after Anita Cobby's murder, Raymond Paterson, 35, of Tivoli Place, Doonside allowed two of the Murphy brothers to stay in his house. Gary and Mick Murphy stayed at his home for the night and told him 'they had mutilated and killed a woman at Prospect.' He did not inform police, he later said, because he was scared.

Days later, Paterson said, Gary Murphy had returned with another person (whom police later discovered was John Travers), borrowed his car and dumped and burnt the stolen car used in the murder. Paterson was charged with being an accessory to murder after the fact, but at least he gave police vital information in the murder investigation. At that time, the police did not know that Gary Murphy was involved in the disposal of the stolen car.

Detectives raided a number of houses before police zeroed in on a townhouse at Tari Way, Glenfield, in Sydney's southwest, on the night of

26 February 1986. Teenager Mavis Saunders was related to the Murphys through the marriage of her sister to one of the other Murphy brothers and had previously had a relationship with Gary Murphy. It was Gary who sought her out to harbour him and his brother Mick. Saunders was staying at the home of 24-year-old Debra McAskill and her six-year-old daughter at the time 'to sort out some personal issues'.

When McAskill, who was two weeks overdue in her second pregnancy, discovered the two men staying at her home were wanted for the murder of Anita Cobby, she said she was so scared for herself and her six-year-old daughter that she didn't know what to do. She told Saunders to tell them to go.

Walking her daughter to school shortly after the discovery, McAskill confided in a friend what was happening in her home. Her friend had called briefly at her house earlier that day and the Murphy brothers had hurried upstairs. The following day, McAskill's brother and his girlfriend arrived, causing the Murphys to hide upstairs again and look out the window. McAskill didn't let her brother inside because she didn't know how the Murphys would react and she didn't want her brother to get hurt. It was her brother who notified police that something was wrong, and she was very glad he did so.

Mick and Gary Murphy were arrested just before 10pm at the Glenfield townhouse. Ian Kennedy, who was in charge of the operation, smashed through the front door with colleague Kevin Raue. Mick Murphy was sitting in the lounge with McAskill's daughter on his lap, watching TV. Kennedy instructed Mick Murphy to quickly get down on the ground. Gary Murphy ran out through the back door and was tackled into a fence by a member of the Police Tactical Response Group. Newsmen on the scene filmed Gary's arrest by detectives, his face grazed and jeans soiled with his own urine.

Debra McAskill and Mavis Saunders were arrested and later charged with being accessories to murder after the fact. 'They told me they had only stolen the car,' McAskill told detectives. 'I was worried all the time because one had already been in gaol and escaped.' When Saunders was asked why she let the men stay with her when she knew they were wanted for murder, the naïve 19-year-old replied that as an Aboriginal woman she could not deny the men shelter. McAskill's daughter was taken by Youth and Community Services, and the two women were later released on bail until the matter went to court the following year.

When the two men were taken to Blacktown Police Station, another angry crowd was waiting for them. The investigation was coming to an emotional conclusion. Even NSW Premier Neville Wran had changed his tune about 'remaining calm'. 'Hanging is too good for them,' he said in a press conference, before firmly rejecting the suggestion of reintroducing the death penalty in NSW.

According to Gary Murphy's record of interview, Mick Murphy and John Travers first saw Anita Cobby walking on Newton Road that night. 'We were just going to grab her handbag until John said, "Let's take her with us." Travers and Michael Murdoch dragged her into the car', he said, and Mick Murphy and John Travers began sexually assaulting her. Gary Murphy denied killing Mrs Cobby, but admitted to forcing her to perform oral sex. At the same time, his brother Mick Murphy was raping her from behind.

'Mick Murphy just went berserk on her,' Gary Murphy stated. '… any way he could, and he was belting her up all the time. All of us were saying things like "we're going to fuck the pants off you." I said it myself,' he admitted. 'It was Mick Murphy who told Travers to cut her throat,' Gary confirmed. Gary heard his brother tell Travers, 'Trawney, do your thing.'

Following his arrest, Mick Murphy started talking to the detectives in the car heading back to Blacktown. Asked why he didn't stop John Travers from murdering Anita Cobby, Murphy told Detective Sergeant Ian Kennedy, 'I didn't want her to be killed; he's a maniac. It's his fault. I told him not to kill her. He's a fucking lunatic. I just wanted to piss off.'

In by far the most detailed record of interview, Mick Murphy gave a full account of the crime, but he too was careful to limit his own involvement. After several hours drinking at Doonside Hotel on the Sunday night, Travers had driven to Windsor with the four co-accused, looking to buy drugs. Driving back into Blacktown, they needed money for petrol and when they saw Anita Cobby walking down the road, 'John just saw her and wanted her.' Travers and Murdoch dragged her into the car, Murphy said. She pleaded with them that she was married and was menstruating, but was told to shut up before Travers punched her hard three times to stop her screaming. Les then 'lent over the back and punched her in the head'.

'John and Mick [Murdoch] started ripping her clothes off before raping her,' Mick Murphy said. Interestingly, the others said it was Travers and Mick Murphy who conducted the first rape. 'They then bought $15 worth of petrol while Travers threatened her with the knife,' he continued, 'telling her not to say nothing, to not scream …'

Mick Murphy told the detectives how his brother Les and Michael Murdoch argued about who would have sex with Anita Cobby at Reen Road. Les, Travers and Murdoch dragged her through the barbed wire fence and walked her down the paddock – 'I think Murdoch had hold of her hair,' he said – before Travers pushed her to the ground. Mick Murphy maintained that he watched the other four try and have sex with her different ways. It was a feeble lie.

Afterwards, and despite Murphy's 'protests', Travers said he was going to cut Anita Cobby's throat. 'We jumped in the car and John came running up with blood all over him,' Murphy said. 'He said, "I cut her throat ... I think I cut a couple of her fingers off 'cause she put her hand up." Travers said, "It's me first one."'

Mick [Murdoch] asked him what it felt like. He said, "Like nothing."'

Later, when the detectives took Mick and Gary Murphy on their respective run-arounds, police held a large media contingent at bay at the top of Reen Road. Graham Rosetta and Tony Waters took Gary Murphy to the paddock where Anita Cobby's body was found. Rosetta pointed out the spot where the body had been lying.

'Is that all her blood?' Gary Murphy asked, looking at a stained area of grass. When Rosetta said it was, Murphy replied, 'Shit, she must have bled.'

Rosetta asked Gary Murphy where he was standing when he heard Mick Murphy tell Travers to 'do your thing'. Murphy pointed to a spot about ten metres away. When asked what Travers did then, Gary Murphy said 'he went back to her' while the others ran to the car.

By mid-morning both Murphy brothers were charged with a raft of offences, including murder. Driving back to Blacktown, another public demonstration greeted the detectives, who later observed that both Gary and Mick Murphy were visibly shaken by the community anger. Journalist Norm Lipson, reporting on Channel 7 News, described the crowd as a 'lynch mob.'

Had they got hold of the men, he said, the crowd would have 'strung them up from the nearest telegraph pole.'

At Blacktown, you could feel the mood of the community. 'It was ugly, murderous,' said Anita's father Garry Lynch. 'The community was outraged that such a thing could happen and that's why they were demonstrating. We were suffering with shock and grief, but we knew that people were thinking of us. They were angry because such a thing should happen here. Why can't we walk on our footpath without being [scared]?'

At 1pm on Thursday, 27 February, Mick and Gary Murphy were taken to Blacktown Court where the police prosecutor presented the evidence against them and successfully argued against bail. Michael Patrick Murphy, age 33, unemployed and of no fixed address and Gary Stephen Murphy, 28, unemployed of Debbie Way, Toongabbie, were refused bail and remanded in custody.

'By 3pm, after working 31 hours straight, we knocked off for the day,' recalls Ian Kennedy. The team of detectives worked 22 days straight, amassing 140 hours of overtime. 'Suffice to say, I – like the other investigators working on the case – was exhausted,' says Garry Heskett.

In the following months, detectives prepared briefs of evidence for the Coroner's Court hearing and ensuing trial. It was time the detectives moved on to other investigations that were still on their books, but the Anita Cobby case would not let go of them so easily.

CHAPTER NINE

THE COMMITTAL

On 28 April 1986, Sydney Hospital unveiled a plaque in honour of Anita Cobby in its chapel. In a modest service attended by Garry and Grace Lynch, former patient Paul Burbidge, 17, paid tribute to Mrs Cobby. 'I was proud to have known such a beautiful lady as Anita,' the former patient from Coffs Harbour Hospital said. 'She was a warm and sensitive human being.'

***Sydney Morning Herald*, 29 April 1986**

Following their arrest, all five offenders appeared before State Coroner Magistrate Derrick Hand at Westmead Coroner's Court on Thursday, 27 February 1986. This is where a magistrate hears all the evidence to decide if, in his opinion, there is sufficient evidence to commit offenders for trial. John Travers, Michael Murdoch and Les Murphy were first presented at Westmead. Earlier that day, Mick and Gary Murphy had made their first appearance at Blacktown Court after being captured the previous day.

Security was heightened at both venues. The Police TRG (Tactical Response Group) escorted Travers, Michael Murdoch and Les Murphy to the court and provided a wall between the public and the men being charged. There had been death threats towards the accused and there were real fears for their safety, particularly after the hostile reception at Blacktown Local Court the previous week. Given the strength of feeling in the community, it was unclear just how far a member of the community might go to get to them.

Across from the Westmead Coroner's Court, a dummy dressed in overalls was hung by a noose from one of the hospital buildings with a sign 'Give Anita's killers a free operation (without aesthetic)'. Anita Cobby, of course, had been a nurse.

It was also the first time Garry Lynch saw the men who had murdered his daughter. His wife Grace and daughter Kathryn did not attend the committal hearing, but Garry was supported by family friend Anne King and her son Martin, who was a former boyfriend of Anita's.

Anne King later wrote, 'The perpetrators were brought into the [Westmead Coroner's] court in a paddy wagon and my son, Garry and myself were there and the crowd went wild. They brought them in the back door, through the security gates, and the perpetrators were screaming things out the back of the van. The crowd was going just as hard back at them.'

The Westmead Court was packed; there wasn't a spare seat in the house. Lawyers for the five men applied for their cases to be heard separately, but the coroner refused the request. They would all be tried together.

'Travers, Murdoch and Murphy refused to look at me,' Magistrate Derrick Hand later recalled. Their heads were bowed, as if they were ashamed, but it was clear to everyone in court that they weren't ashamed at all. 'Instead, I saw them glance around the court, their demeanour cocky. They appeared to not take any notice of what was going on, as if they were saying, "So why are we here then?"'

The charges were read out and the three men were remanded for trial. Shortly after, Mick and Gary Murphy arrived in handcuffs after their appearance at Blacktown Court. After a brief formality, they joined the other three in the holding cells.

It was obvious, however, that Westmead Coroner's Court was not big enough to host the committal hearing for the five accused. There were also security issues, not so much the fear the men would break out but that someone would break in and harm them, so it was agreed to transfer the venue closer to the city to Glebe Coroner's Court on Parramatta Road and reconvene in six months' time. Although none of the men applied for bail, Magistrate Hand formally refused bail.

On Monday, 23 June 1986, the five accused appeared for the reconvened committal hearing in Court One of the Glebe Coroner's Court on Parramatta Road, Sydney. Security again was paramount, with the TRG surrounding the courthouse, sniffer dogs in tow, security checkpoints set up and a metal detector installed. Grace and Garry Lynch, again supported by Anne King, attended all eight days at Glebe Coroner's Court where evidence of what happened to Anita was tabled by police. It was necessary to support Anita's name and reputation, they said.

'Anita's parents conducted themselves with dignity and pride throughout the hearing,' Derrick Hand later observed, 'displaying an inner strength that most of us do not know we possess until we need it.'

There, Grace Lynch faced the men on trial. 'They looked weak,' she remarked to her husband, and she was disgusted that 'they could only have found strength in numbers, and must have felt "big and tough" after drinking a few beers and driving around in a stolen car.' Of the ringleader, John Travers, Garry Lynch later made note of his 'dead eyes.'

During the committal hearing, a small woman with grey, frizzy hair and wearing thongs approached the Lynch Family. It was Rose Murdoch, Michael Murdoch's mother. Garry Lynch later wrote, 'It was sad because Murdoch's mother was the only representative of any of them that came to the proceedings. She was there right through both the committal and the trial. During the committal at the Coroner's Court, she approached Peg to say how sorry she was for what had happened, but we were asked not to get involved or it could be embarrassing later on.'

The five men were dressed in jeans, casual shirts and sandshoes, and looked very much the same as when they first appeared 'smirking and smiling at each other, even winking'. Derrick Hand later observed, 'They looked around the courtroom as if they didn't have a care in the world … they showed no respect for anyone, including themselves.'

Police Detective Sergeant Allan Ezzy, the police prosecutor, called his first witness, Detective Sergeant Ian Kennedy, to outline the police's case against the five. In clinical detail, Kennedy detailed how Anita Cobby was abducted off a Blacktown Street, assaulted and robbed, then pack raped by the five men. He then described how the men later agreed that she should be killed because she had seen their faces and knew their names, and John Travers had cut her throat with a large hunting knife.

The following day, lawyers for the five accused protested when Crown Prosecutor Allan Ezzy sought to tender colour photos of Anita Cobby's body that had been taken by the police photographer at the crime scene. It was an old argument, even for 1986. The photos were too explicit, the lawyers said, too prejudicial to their clients and far too emotive to show to the jury. Hand allowed the photos to be entered into evidence because they were relevant to the case. The images also displayed the stark horror of the crimes committed against the victim.

Ezzy then proposed that a post mortem report by Chief Medical Officer Dr Joe Malouf be read aloud in court. The suggestion was immediately greeted by a chorus of 'no' from counsel representing the defendants and the report was tendered but not read. At this point, Grace Lynch was led out of the court by one of the detectives to protect her from the details, but Garry Lynch remained in court.

Dr Malouf referred to the crime scene photos as he spoke. 'The uppermost of the severe lacerations at the front of the neck extended from below the angle of the left jaw, across the front of the neck and behind the angle of the right jaw, severing the ear,' he said. The cut was clean at the edge but jagged at the base and, in Malouf's opinion, the instrument was then 'sawed backwards and forwards, destroying the tissue.'

'Anita Cobby', he said, 'would have died within two minutes'.

As Dr Malouf explained, there were numerous cuts and scratches on Anita's legs and across her back where she had been dragged through the barbed wire fence at the paddock. She had been raped, both vaginally and anally, and there were cuts to her anus. Her nose had been broken, causing bruising to both eyes, but her eye socket had also been broken by a 'blow of considerable force.'

A knife with a serrated edge, almost 30cm in length from tip to handle, caused the injury, Malouf said. Although the murder weapon was never found, lawyers for Michael Murdoch successfully protested the tendering of a similar 'Rambo-style' knife in a leather pouch as evidence. Detective Senior Constable Paul Hamilton of the Penrith Scientific Branch had been given the knife, along with other possessions allegedly belonging to Murdoch and Travers, at Blacktown Police Station. Tests for blood had produced positive results but experts were not able to conclude if the blood was human and so the nexus between that knife and the alleged crime was not established. There was no nexus, however, between this particular knife and the actual crime and so it could not be tendered as evidence.

In cross-examining Malouf's testimony, one of the lawyers for John Travers detailed the injuries to Anita Cobby's throat and asked if the cows could have caused those injuries. The question received the scorn it deserved from the public gallery, and incredulity from the Lynch family, and Magistrate Hand called for order.

No, said Malouf, the cows did not cause the injuries.

A steady stream of witnesses took the stand – Garry Lynch, the detectives on the case, the McGaughey siblings from Newton Road, neighbours of Travers' family at Doonside and finally 'Miss X'. When the various detectives tendered records of interviews for the five men, defence counsel tried to intimate that members of the police had assaulted the defendants and fabricated statements.

'They did try to retract their confessions,' former Detective Kevin Raue later remarked, 'which is not uncommon, by saying that they had been forced to make them.' It was the accused's only defence – they were bashed by police who forced them to sign confessions. Individual semen tests had been 'inconclusive' so there was no forensic evidence to prove which of the men had had sex with the victim, but Raue and the other detectives took the stand and said the defence lawyers' assertions were 'totally false'.

Three weeks after Mick and Gary Murphy were arrested, Travers' next door neighbour came forward and told police that on the night Anita Cobby was murdered, she observed some men in the backyard standing around a fire, drinking beer and talking. The fire was 'burning intensely' and a lot of smoke was coming from it. Mrs Maxine Greensmith of Tich Place, Doonside, had known John Travers for five years and the other men for about a month. Michael Murdoch and Les and Gary Murphy had each used her phone, she said. Miss Greensmith later added that Lisa Travers was with them, although she was originally unsure of this point. She later admitted that she was 'scared' of Lisa Travers.

Mrs Greensmith also told the court that some weeks before the Cobby murder she had seen John Travers with a knife and a bleeding lamb at a party in the house next door. Her daughter had alerted her to the scene, and Mrs Greensmith had gone to the back window of her home and saw Travers 'kneeling on the back lawn with his right arm around the lamb's neck and his left leg over its legs.'

A party was in progress that night, and Michael Murdoch and Mick and Gary Murphy were there with their girlfriends and others. Asked during cross-examination what Travers was doing to the lamb, Mrs Greensmith replied, 'Well, the throat had been cut already and blood was just coming out – not gushing out, just flowing out and he held the knife up and he went to cut the lamb towards the stomach and I just ran into the bathroom.'

She said Travers held the lamb's head back when he cut its throat.

Mrs Greensmith said that two weeks after the late night 'fire' incident, Les Murphy came into her house to use her telephone. After hanging up he said, 'Do you know what they are trying to pin me with?'

'What?' she asked.

'The Anita Cobby murder … yeah, they want me in for a blood test and to hypnotise me.'

When Miss Greensmith suggested he should cooperate with the police, he replied, 'You know, I never went out that night. The car didn't go out and if the car doesn't go out, I don't go out.'

Murphy urged Mrs Greensmith to tell 'the Ds' that he had been at home the night of the murder. 'He kept at me over and over about telling the police that he was home.'

Although she admitted she only came forward after details of the men's capture were reported in the media, Mrs Greensmith denied that media reports of the arrests had influenced her testimony. Asked under cross-examination why she didn't report the incident to police sooner, she said, 'I had known John Travers for five years. I was a very frightened woman.'

In a sensational final day of the hearing, Miss X took the stand to give her evidence. Everyone associated with the five men knew who she was, but having been placed in witness protection, her identity had been supressed. The 25-minute tape recording of the conversation was largely inaudible (interestingly, a transcript of the recording was tendered as an exhibit but not read out aloud.) 'You could have heard a pin drop in that courtroom,' Hand observed. 'At intervals during the playing of the tape, the three Murphy brothers appeared very amused.'

Their mood was to change when the full details of the conversation with Miss X was revealed. Travers admitted to cutting Anita Cobby's throat and named all four co-accused as complicit in her abduction, assault, rape and murder. It was damning evidence. Under cross-examination, Miss X admitted that she was a heroin user and would be applying for the reward money on offer.

As Miss X left the witness stand, the five men in the dock unleashed a torrent of abuse. All of the men sprang to their feet with Travers lunging at her, yelling, 'You bitch, you fuckin' bitch, I'll get you!' Ian Kennedy had anticipated the move, however, and positioned himself and a couple of other police officers between the men and Miss X to protect her. The attack rattled Miss X. 'We thought she wouldn't come back in and give evidence,' says Kennedy, 'and I'm sure Travers did too, but it backfired on him. It made her more determined.'

The lawyer for Gary Murphy, an American, provided a brief moment of levity during proceedings when he argued that, in arresting Gary Murphy, detectives had failed to read the accused his Miranda rights ('you have the right to remain silent ...'). Although the wording doesn't differ too much under Australian law, police do not have to make someone aware of their rights during an arrest, as their American counterparts do when charging an offender.

On 1 July 1986, Travers, Murdoch and Mick and Les Murphy were committed to stand trial for 'kidnapping, sexual assault, robbery and murder'. Gary Murphy was committed to trial on the following day after his lawyer had asked for a one day adjournment to attend to a family matter. The lawyers defending Gary Murphy had tried everything to separate his client's actions from the rest of the group. It was conceded that Gary Murphy had taken part in the abduction and robbery of the victim, but his lawyers maintained he was not involved in her sexual assault or murder.

Even these admissions would change for the trial.

GARRY HESKETT REMEMBERS

Garry Heskett was a member of the Australian Army for six years, functioning as an infantry soldier and seeing active war experience in Vietnam. After his service, he became an ambulance officer with the NSW Ambulance Service before joining the NSW Police. He spent 25 years as a cop, the majority as a homicide detective.

Garry witnessed firsthand 'the visible as well as the private suffering caused by the impact of careless or deliberate actions that human beings may wish to inflict upon other human beings.' The closure people seek is often never to be found.

At the time he was asked to return to Blacktown in February 1986, Heskett was investigating Yugoslav crime and the stabbing murder of two Vietnamese males in the Cabramatta district. In his own words, 'my plate was full'. As a Detective Constable, he was the junior member on the task force.

'I was very proud of the fact that I didn't make an application to go to the Homicide Squad in the city. I was picked, and that's what was done in those days … like representative footballers being scouted, unlike today where you have to apply for promotion and then fight appeals to keep your place. Back then, you had to prove that you could work within the team. Current police officers may disagree, but I still think it's the best way of doing things.

'Blacktown was a very robust area and I was very busy as a detective there. There wasn't a time when two or three times a week detectives weren't off on raids. Early morning search warrants, locking up armed robbers or breaking and entering merchants … you name it, we were dealing with all facets of crime in the Blacktown area.'

Heskett's unit covered the Mt Druitt area, as well as Blacktown, so they worked in close liaison with Mt Druitt and Penrith detectives. 'There is little job satisfaction for the average police officer who works in the lower socio-economic areas. We investigate mostly economic crime, which is crime associated with minority and disadvantaged groups who are attempting to inoculate themselves from poverty.'

Heskett was so busy that, looking back, he says it was as if he was never home. 'Not many people outside that policing circle would appreciate the close bond those guys developed working so closely together. It was like a rugby league team … we still have annual reunions. I could be wrong, but we could be the only detective's office in NSW that continues to have reunions more than 30 years on – those fellows who worked out of that office in the four to five years I was there, from 1980 to 1985, still have a reunion.

'We knew this investigation was about the real world and about the real things that humans could do to each other. We knew there would not be divine intervention and that if the matter was solved, it would be through a combination of hard work and a few good breaks. We didn't talk in clichés, and although we were part of an elite group, the Homicide Squad, there were none of us who held any idealistic notions about investigating the matter. In any event, even if we did, the local detectives soon reminded us of our place … and without the cooperation of the local police, and the local population of both ordinary citizens and those on the other side of the fence, we were not going to get very far with this matter.

'In the initial investigation, we were looking for potentially two vehicles so we started up a police running sheet for both and pursued that course of inquiry until they were exhausted. Inquiries were coming from telephone tips left, right and centre, so you wrote them down and followed them through. There were lots of running sheets and each line of inquiry had to be exhausted. That was the hard yards in policing ... get on to the next line on inquiry. As we moved through the investigation, we had meetings and briefings and we started to pick up on threads and theories, which often lead us towards a different direction.'

The first thing they learned was that a group of men had taken the woman off the street.

'I had not come across the perpetrators before. I locked up a lot of crooks in Blacktown but not the Murphy brothers. I'd heard of them, but also not encountered Travers or Murdoch.

'When we were on the hunt for the Murphy brothers, we went to Murphy's family home and spoke to his mother Dulcie. We searched the place from back to front and upside down and there was nothing there so we decided to go to his sister's place at Granville. We went to two places after that and they said he wasn't there. Gary and Mick were being harboured by two women at Glenfield.

'We had John Travers locked up on warrants, so we knew it would only be a matter of time before we pieced it all together. We made sure everything was spot on. We had continual briefings ... there were to be no stuff ups and we had to be sure we were all on the same page. All of Australia was looking on us. There was a lot of community anxiety and media hype. It held the front page of the old Sun newspaper 14 days straight.'

'We didn't solve the case because there was organisational or political obligations to do so ... we were all decent people and we cared what happened. We were hard ... but we cared about what we did because of our working class beginnings ... that spirit of cooperation rather than being competitive with each other.

'Their behaviour at trial showed them the five offenders what they were ... immature, killers,' says Heskett. 'I have no idea why they acted that way, but there was no remorse, no decency and no respect for anything. I'd never seen that before and in my time at Homicide and I had dealt with many murders.

'Travers pleaded guilty; the rest pleaded not guilty, but they were all part of it. Just because they didn't actually cut Anita's throat doesn't mean they weren't complicit in her murder. They held her down and they raped her … they had a common purpose.'

'A lot of crimes get compared to the Cobby case – the Janine Balding case two years later, for example – but it stands alone as a benchmark. It's an embarrassment really that it is the benchmark for murder. What does it say about society? I worked on many other cases – some equally as poignant, such as the abduction and murder of Ebony Simpson in 1992 – but none had the national impact of the Cobby case in so far as the legislative and community changes that were bought about.

'Truth is, sentence was one result … do the crime, do the correct bloody time … and no paroles of good behaviour. "Life means life" … we got that changed.'

'Some people have said to me over the years,' Heskett says, "Did you know the Murphys were out?" I'd say, "Piss off, they're still in gaol." Even though we're out of policing now, we'd be notified if that was ever to happen. The whole country would be on alert. Australia would rise as a nation if they did get released.

'Baker and Crump have been in gaol for more than 40 years with no sign of a release. They kicked up to the prison padre saying they had found God and should be released and shown some leniency, some form of parole … the husband of Virginia Morse has to go and plead his case every time parole comes up.

'All homicide cases are important, but it wasn't a case where we could say "I've had enough, I'm going home." We solved it and we did a bloody good job'.

'There was an old school protocol at work. Ian "Speed" Kennedy was the boss and Graham "Rosie" Rosetta was the Detective Sergeant out at Blacktown. They were the boys who ran the show and the rest of us fell in behind them. Today you would be walking around with medals on your chest … in my day you were lucky to get a mention in the police bulletin but that's OK. The only pat on the back you needed is the one written up in your police file.

'I won the Police Officer of the Year in my later days in policing, because the community knew me. I made myself known to the shop owners and local people … kept hoodlums off streets and the drugs down … but it's a different world today. Policing has changed.

'Today, police are handcuffed by consultants and PR agencies foreign to the police service … my message to them is don't let consultants handcuff your humanity. Often fear, unrecognised and unacknowledged, can act as an inhibitor on our own actions, causing us to "stick to the book" rather than acting on instinct and/or intuition. We should not let our common sense, humour and humanity be handcuffed by consultants, fashions and agendas foreign to the pure notion of police service.

'Garry Lynch was a good man, and I spent a lot of time with them over the years, particularly with his wife Grace and Anne King, a solid friend, who stuck with them through all that time. During the trial at Darlinghurst, I used to take them up to Oxford Street for a coffee when something nasty was coming up in court and they didn't need to hear it. They were lovely people.

Garry would take the role of family spokesman with Grace always by his side. 'During both the trials and being the junior member of the homicide team, from time to time I was given the task of looking after them … I would often take then to a coffee shop in Oxford Street when I knew technical or nasty material was being produced in court. We got close during those times, and when it was all over we went our separate ways.'

'I realise that whilst at the mortuary and standing beside Garry trying my best to remain detached and professional … that Grace, his lifetime partner should have been beside him so they could comfort each other. Grace has told me so many times that she should have been there. There was nothing strange in my thinking and belief at the time, for I had been raised that women should be protected … underestimating the immense strength of women. I came to know Grace as a woman of remarkable strength and courage. When understanding Grace, you begin to understand where Anita Cobby's tenacity, strength and determination came from.'

Ten years after the crime, Garry Heskett was developing an Investigators Course for the Macarthur Police District in Southwest Sydney on behalf of the NSW Police Academy. He went to the local mall to see long distance runner and local member Pat Farmer set off on a fundraising run. Garry and Grace Lynch were there and they greeted Heskett like a long lost friend. That initial re-connection in early 1996 was the catalyst for many lectures by Garry and Grace Lynch as well as many others of the Homicide Victims Support Group.

'I never realised the impact I had on their lives – not only me, of course, but they felt that way about all the police involved in the investigation – to keep tabs on my career the way they had was overwhelming to say the least.'

In 2001, Heskett received a request from Con Gouriotis, on behalf of Garry and Grace Lynch, to become part of the curatorial for the exhibition Anita and Beyond. 'I was hesitant and really had no desire to be involved but realised Garry and Grace needed my support – as they had supported me over the years.

One of the mandatory lectures Garry Heskett developed in the Investigators Course was on the Victim of Crime Support Group which highlighted the work of the Victims Support Policy Statement and the NSW Government's Charter of Victim's Rights. Garry and Grace Lynch were invited as guest lecturers ten years to the day since their involvement in the original case. Both were full of enthusiasm and wanted to be involved in the course.

Garry Heskett retired after 25 years of operational police work in November 2003. For the previous seven years, he had fought PTSD from his time in Vietnam and depression from his years in the police force. 'From an early age, I was able to insulate myself against the stress and anxiety that these violent and brutal incidents inflict upon many,' he says, but in the end, the changing nature of policing wore him down.

'Apart from the bodies, I'd had too many adrenalin rushes,' he later wrote in Forged by War: Australians in Combat and Back Home (edited by Gina Lennox). 'I continued work but I was nervous and agitated … changes in the police force culture [were] aggravating my problems. I still had enough sanity and health to reinvent myself.'

'The Cobby matter always comes up,' he says, 'There are anniversaries and memorials, so it will never be forgotten.'

Nor should it be.

CHAPTER TEN

The Trial

'The trial was horrific ... we'd go away physically and emotionally drained, dreading the next day's revelations. The court room had the worst acoustics of any building in the whole of the Commonwealth ... and everybody all talked in such subdued tones that we seldom actually heard anything anybody said. We went there nearly every day for three months to represent Anita, to ensure she would not be seen as a nameless victim and also for the latter part of it to support the police when they were being pilloried by the defence.
We began to wonder who was on trial.'
Garry Lynch

The trial of John Travers, Michael Murdoch and Mick, Gary and Les Murphy started on Monday, 16 March 1987, at Court No.5 at the NSW Supreme Downing Street Court Complex in Darlinghurst. Justice Alan Maxwell was the presiding judge for the trial, Miss Beverley Dalley was his senior associate and Mr RM Shumach his tipstaff, or administrative support. Once again, the court was heavily guarded by specially implemented security measures and armed police.

In a sensational start to the trial the opening day, however, John Travers pleaded guilty to kidnapping, sexually assaulting and murdering Anita Cobby. He was remanded in custody for sentencing when the trial of the other four was completed.

The Crown alleged that although John Travers was the one who murdered Anita Cobby, the four accused were equally guilty, having agreed that she had to be killed because she 'saw their faces and heard their names.' Through their legal representatives, the accused contested the veracity of the police interviews and other aspects of the case. Les Murphy stated that he was drunk and did not take part in the rape and murder. Michael Murdoch opted for a similar defence while Gary Murphy claimed he was not even there on the night. Their lies would be found out through the skilful work of Crown Prosecutor Allan Saunders and the evidence presented by the task force of detectives.

The first of 43 witnesses listed to give evidence in the first two weeks was Garry Lynch, who provided background for his daughter Anita and her last known movements. That evening, however, the Sydney newspaper *The Sun* published on its front page a photograph of Travers alongside the headline in bold type: ANITA MURDER MAN GUILTY. A report about the opening of the trial inside the newspaper identified Mick Murphy as 'a gaol escapee of no fixed address.'

The following day, the trial was dramatically aborted. Mr Bill Hosking, QC for Mick Murphy, said there was 'grave, unnecessary and irreparable prejudice in the [newspaper] report' and asked the judge to select another jury to ensure his client received a fair trial. After a brief adjournment, the judge brought in the four defendants and cited the offending article. He said it was 'with great reluctance' that he had made the decision to discharge the jury.

Justice Maxwell then agreed to Mr Hosking's submission that a fresh trial start the next week, rather than the following day as the judge initially proposed. A jury of seven men and five women were empanelled for the second jury, which was reduced to eleven when one woman withdrew because of health issues. When the Court reconvened on 23 March, an application was made to Justice Maxwell on behalf of each of the accused to adjourn the trial for another six months. The application was based upon the publication in *The Sun* on 16 March, and upon the further publicity of 17 and 18 March, but this application was denied.

There was a 'smugness' about the accused. The four men were seen 'glaring at the crowd and prosecutors' and 'showed no remorse for the crime they committed'. When Justice Maxwell was describing the injuries to Anita Cobby, Mick Murphy gave out an audible laugh and was rebuked by the judge in front of the jury.

During the 54 days of trial, the defence lawyers 'were ruthless in their condemnation of the police', particularly the leader of the investigation, Detective Sergeant Ian Kennedy. Bill Hosking, for Mick Murphy, asked that Kennedy be cross-examined in the absence of the jury in relations to his client's arrest at Glenfield on 26 February. Hosking put it to Kennedy that his client's record of interview 'was a fabrication' and that Murphy had been 'bashed and kicked', leaving a mark on his client's face.

Kennedy denied the statement was a 'work of fiction' and said that any allegation that the accused was bashed or kicked was 'a lie'. Kennedy 'strenuously' denied that Mick Murphy had been assaulted by other detectives during his record of interview. He did concede, however, that the description tendered at Blacktown Court of Mick Murphy 'struggling 'or 'resisting arrest' when the detective had the accused on the floor at the Glenfield townhouse was an exaggeration, but only because he said he pushed Murphy's head down with his foot with such force that it prevented 'anything that could have been seen as resisting arrest.'

Kennedy told the court that the interview with Murphy was not taped because 'to his knowledge there are no tape recorders available in the NSW Police Department for taping records of interview, and there were certainly none at Blacktown that night'.

Detective Inspector Kevin Parsons, duty inspector on the night of Mick Murphy's arrest, confirmed a mark on Mick Murphy's face was actually a mat burn. 'It was not a serious injury that I considered was the result of an assault,' Parson told the court. Although he did not specifically ask Murphy about the mark on his face, he had asked Murphy if he had any complaints about the manner in which the record of interview was conducted and Murphy had signed his record of interview 'freely and voluntarily' without Ian Kennedy and Kevin Raue being present.

Detective Garry Heskett said Les Murphy had 'voluntarily indicated to police the sites of various alleged crimes on his 21 February run-around and had 'no problem whatsoever' understanding questions put to him by Detective Sergeant Raue during his record of interview. Several times during the interview, Raue had asked Murphy how he felt and Murphy said words to the effect: 'I'm glad it's all over …. [and to] get it off my chest.' They removed Murphy's handcuffs and even got him a cup of coffee, Heskett told the court, and he described Murphy as 'compliant' and even 'happy'.

During Detective Sergeant Ray Kilburn's evidence, in which a tape recording of the discussion between Miss X and Michael Murdoch was played, Justice Maxwell explained to the jury that the tape recorded evidence was admissible evidence only against Michael Murdoch and not the Murphy brothers (Travers having already pled guilty). Miss X agreed she was wired for sound when she spoke to Murdoch at about 11pm on 23 February the previous year, but apart from not disclosing the tape recorder was on her body, she had not intended to deceive him in regards to what she asked him.

On 8 May, after six weeks, the Crown ended its case.

A week later, the jury was taken on a 'jury view' of the crime scene. The jury left the courtroom complex and, under the supervision of the Sherriff's Office and Court attendants, were bused to Reen Road. A specially sworn-in sheriff's officer showed the jurors where Anita Cobby had been dragged from the car on the unsealed road, through the barbed wire fence, into the wooded paddock and finally to where she had been murdered. Justice Alan Maxwell, two shorthand reporters, various detectives, uniformed police and the legal teams for both sides made the journey in private cars. Two helicopters circled overhead with the media kept well away.

The trip back to court was made in relative silence.

The defence case for Michael Murdoch ended after just 15 minutes. Under the law, he chose to address the jury rather than give evidence on which he could be cross-examined. Murdoch stood in the dock, flanked by several police officers, sipping from a glass of water. Wearing a light-grey suit and horn-rimmed glasses, he looked more like a young school teacher than a man fighting a raft of charges. Murdoch said that he was at Travers' home in Doonside when the others arrived in the stolen car. The group drove towards Windsor and while Travers visited a friend of Murdoch's brother, 'the rest of us drank beer and smoked marijuana in the car for about 15 minutes.'

When they grabbed Anita Cobby off the street, Murdoch said he shifted from the back seat to the front of the car to help Les Murphy look in the girl's bag for money. After filling the car with petrol, Travers instructed Mick Murphy to drive to Reen Road.

'I never at any time laid a hand on Mrs Cobby,' Michael Murdoch said. 'I didn't have sex with Mrs Cobby in any way …' He also maintained that some of the answers he gave the police were 'not true because I was scared.' He concluded his unsworn statement thus:

'I would just like to make it clear at this time that … in fact at no time was there any discussion that we were going to abduct Mrs Cobby, let alone rape and murder her. I know I'm guilty for stealing the car, and that I was there and I didn't do nothing about it, but I didn't want her to be abducted and I didn't want her to be raped, and I certainly didn't want her to be murdered. Thank you.'

Gary Murphy was the only defendant to give an alibi defence. Ms Jennifer Betts, of the Office of the Solicitor for Public Prosecutions, told the court that apart from a telephone conversation earlier that day, the only notice she was given that Gary Murphy intended using an alibi defence was in a letter sent three weeks before the trial. Murphy had been drinking at the Doonside Hotel until late at night, he maintained, and had left with a man named Ray Paterson.

'I don't know where I went, I can't remember,' he told the detectives, 'but what I do know is that I was not at a rape or murder.

'I did not rape, I did not murder. I was not there … '

In his unsworn statement to the court, Murphy said he 'hardly knew' John Travers and had never been to Travers' place for a party or barbeque or been present while a sheep was killed. He maintained that he had heard from 'a friend' that he was wanted by police and someone else told him the police would 'shoot him on sight'. When police burst into the townhouse at Glenfield, he ran out of the house because he was scared he would be shot. He ran into a laneway, but there was nowhere to go, he said. A police officer with a shotgun allegedly told him to lie down, which he did. He was then kicked and punched, and struck with the end of the gun, causing him to wet his pants.

This statement could not be cross-examined by the Crown because it was an unsworn statement from the dock. Gary Murphy's version of events was contradicted by Detective Sergeant Alan Moule, a member of the Tactical Response Group, who gave corroborative evidence of seeing Gary Murphy running into a backyard and being tackled by a colleague named Ian Donaldson. Moule said the tackle caused Murphy to collide face first, 'pretty square on' with a paling fence. Murphy was screaming and resisting arrest, but it was only after being assisted to his feet that the abrasions on Murphy's face were noticed. Moule denied that Murphy had been kicked or struck on the head with a shotgun butt.

Detective Sergeant Tony Waters said Gary Murphy had 'freely and voluntarily' given police a record of interview at Blacktown Station on the night of 26 February. Waters said the proposition that another police officer came into the interview room and 'pulled Murphy by the hair at least six times' was ridiculous.

When Gary Murphy was taken to Parklea Gaol after his arrest, a doctor informed him that his jaw was broken. According to medical records from the gaol, his jaw had 'recently been broken in two places' which required his mouth to be wired. While his relatively new team of lawyers put this report forward as evidence of a police bashing, Murphy did not tell his lawyers that his jaw had been broken. The Crown argued that the broken jaw had occurred before his arrest when Murphy got into a fist fight.

At one point in the trial, Les Murphy was absent from court because of injuries he suffered in his cell when a steel door opened without warning. When he finally took the stand, he spent 18 minutes giving his 'side of the story'. He spent scant time talking about the crime, other than that he was 'off his face' that day. He maintained that he 'did not have sex with the girl' and that although he saw Travers covered in blood incredibly, he did not know Travers had killed her.

Older brother Mick said from the dock, 'It was a terrible thing that John Travers done to Mrs Cobby,' mispronouncing her name 'Cobey'. 'He must have been insane ... At no time did I touch Mrs Cobby at all.' Like his brother Gary, Mick spent most of his time detailing a litany of alleged mistreatment by the police.

The jury retired on 9 June 1987. After nearly nine hours of deliberation, they informed the judge that they had not yet reached a verdict and were empanelled overnight. The following morning, sometime after 10 o'clock, they reached their verdict. The court opened the upstairs section of the public gallery to take in the overflow of media people and spectators. There was an air of expectation not only in the courtroom, but also around the country with news services covering the verdict with live crosses to the NSW Supreme Court.

At 10.40 am the jury foreman replied 'guilty' to the names of the four men in the dock. Wild applause and cheering erupted from a packed No.5 Court at Darlinghurst. 'I have never heard thunder and applause in that building,' said journalist Julia Sheppard, who would later write a book about the case. 'The floor shook, people were clapping and cheering. Justice Maxwell very quickly got the court to stop and told them it was inappropriate ... but there was just jubilation.'

The Lynches and their supporters embraced each other and cried. Members of the jury were also visibly upset. Even the detectives who worked on the case shed a tear. The trail was faultless, Ian Kennedy says. 'From years of observation, I've decided judges all have their idiosyncrasies – that's why I believe in the jury system – but Justice Maxwell was meticulous. He didn't miss a beat.'

Grace and Garry Lynch were not present for the sentencing of the five men, and asked Anne King to represent them at Court. The Lynch family had given their all to the police, the media and to the trial, and so they decided to get away and stay with friends and 'left the sentencing to the wisdom of Justice Maxwell.'

On 16 June 1987, Andrew Linden, barrister for John Travers, asked for a sentence with a parole period and argued his client was 'not beyond rehabilitation' because he had 'adopted what is still a most unusual course' and pleaded guilty. No complaint had been made of the behaviour of the police, Mr Linden said, adding tellingly, 'what one could say are the usual allegations against police.'

Like those made by Murdoch and the Murphy brothers.

On 19 June, Judge Victor Maxwell declined to grant the killers parole, directing that the file of each man be marked 'never to be released'. The killers were 'worse than animals,' he said. 'Wild animals are given to pack assaults and killings. However, they do so for the purposes of survival … Not so these prisoners. They assaulted in a pack for the purpose of satisfying their lust and killed for the purpose of [avoiding] identification.'

Describing the crime as 'one of the most, if not the most, horrifying physical and sexual assaults I've encountered in my 40 odd years associated with the law', Justice Maxwell declined to specify non-parole periods. If any person was to consider paroling any of them, Justice Maxwell said, 'The executives should grant to the prisoners the same degree of mercy that they bestowed on Anita Lorraine Cobby in Mr Reen's boiler paddock on the night of 2 February 1986.'

Justice Maxwell did not believe Travers' state of mind was a mitigating factor in the murder, nor that he alone was responsible for the murder. All five men got the same sentence. In addition to life sentences for murder, the five prisoners were each convicted of murder (for which the sentence was penal servitude for life), of taking with intent to hold for advantage (for which the sentence was 16 years imprisonment), of assault and robbery, immediately after such robbery using corporal violence wounding the victim (for which the sentence was 17 years imprisonment), of inflicting actual bodily harm with intent to have sexual intercourse (for which the sentence was 12 years imprisonment) and of stealing a car (for which the sentence was five years imprisonment) save for Leslie Murphy, who was sentenced to three years imprisonment.

When Michael Murdoch was led from the court, he looked over his shoulder towards his mother and shrugged his shoulders.

CHAPTER ELEVEN

The Family

'When Anita didn't come home that night, we just presumed she was staying with friends. Later in the evening, I was sitting on my bed with the window open. It was a beautiful, very hot summer night, and I was looking out at the night sky. A three-quarter moon was tinting those billowing clouds. Suddenly one of those clouds transformed into the most evil face I could ever imagine – absolute evil.'

Garry Lynch

By any measure, Garry Lynch lived an extraordinary life. Born in 1918, he led a nomadic existence as a runaway during the 1930s before seeing action in the Middle East during World War II. He later led an artistic, bohemian lifestyle in the post-war years before pursuing his dreams in the remote Kimberley region of Western Australia, where he met his future wife Grace, known as 'Peg', who was a nursing sister. Having joined the Navy as a clerical assistant, Garry became a teacher of technical drawing and later, a graphic designer. The Lynch family later moved to Blacktown in Western Sydney, where Garry and Grace raised two daughters, Anita and Kathryn.

Playing in the family backyard with his sister Cecile as a youngster, Garry Lynch was once struck by lightning during a storm – a metaphor perhaps for what he and his family felt happened to them when their daughter Anita was murdered in 1986 – and later the incident became the title of his autobiography. Garry grew up as a member of a large Catholic Irish family, but his faith in religion pretty much went out the door when Lynch's mother left his father, a struggling alcoholic.

After the war, however, Garry pursued meditation and Eastern Mysticism to relieve the depression he suffered from his war service. He admits that he indulged in too much drinking and gambling, but he learned to control his urges and found the much-needed balance in his life raising two young daughters in Western Sydney. Grace Lynch had her own 'spiritual awakening' the year before their second daughter was born in

1964. Together, Garry and Grace Lynch emanated an air of quiet patience and calmness, qualities that would be sorely tested in the early months of 1986 and in the hard years that followed.

Garry retired from public service in 1978 at the age of 60, and afterwards often went to Lightning Ridge, near Bathurst west of Sydney, to go mining for rare black opal. It was his home away from home, and he stayed there for months at a time. Meanwhile, Grace continued to work as a nurse. Both of Garry's daughters married in their early 20s, as was the fashion of the time, and left the family home. That quiet life changed in February 1986 when Anita's marriage broke up and she was murdered walking home from work one Sunday night.

Even when the detectives knocked on his door to tell him that they had found a body, and that it was more than likely his missing daughter, Garry was just as concerned for the men charged with finding his daughters' murderers. 'I could see they were upset, very agitated, fearful of my reactions and I said to them, "I want you to understand that if this is as bad as it's beginning to look … rest assured that we will see it through, we'll see it through to the very end" and that gave a bit of reassurance that we'd all be able to handle whatever, which we did…

'I remember saying to Peg [Grace],' Garry said, '"We are going to step into a little bit of hell, but bad as it is, there's no avoiding it, we have to face it and persevere with patience to any horror that may be presented to us"… and I think that's what we did.'

Anita's former husband was particularly struggling. 'John came over that afternoon and cried, "If I'd been a better husband this wouldn't have happened."' The Lynches reassured the young man that the only person responsible for the tragedy was the animal who did it. Cobby was 'completely devastated'. After Anita's funeral, he changed his name and lived overseas for several years. 'He went through much suffering and it was a long time before he was able to go on with his life,' Garry observed.

But the grieving father also felt enormous guilt. 'Why wasn't I down there last Sunday, waiting for her?' he chided himself. 'Even if I had sat in the car all flamin' night.'

Grace was 'too numb in those early days – too devastated to cry or feel angry', Garry wrote of that time, while in his own mind 'emotions bubbled up like tidal waves of hate and suspicion'. A friend wrote to them and said that he'd been helped when a loved one died by repeating a mantra over and over again in his mind. Garry and Grace repeated, 'Anita is now radiant and supremely happy with God' and the couple found that the words helped them enormously.

'It was just horrific,' said Grace of that time. 'It's just something I can't imagine anyone doing to another human being. It's just something that's beyond my thinking … We supported each other and our daughter, Kathryn.'

'It was a palpable support,' Garry said. 'You could feel it, you know, you could feel it.'

'We didn't know who had committed the murder,' Grace added. 'We didn't know for three weeks. Everything just stopped … we thought maybe the people who did it would never be caught.'

'There was nothing really to go on,' Grace said. 'We thought this may not ever be solved so we were really very grateful.' Said Garry, '[The police] were honest enough to say "we're in a blind alley here, we don't know exactly where it's leading us but we're pursuing it, we have some facts, as far as we'd call them facts, but we can't share them with you yet" and I said "Well, I appreciate that, I appreciate your frankness …"'

As the days passed, the Lynches took calls from shocked relatives and friends, as well as strangers who had lost members of their own families, and of course the police who continued to drop in and brief the family on the investigation. 'There was no counselling, and we didn't even think of seeking it out,' Garry said. 'What could anyone have done?'

The idea that his daughter was 'in the wrong place at the wrong time' chaffed with Gary. 'She was walking home to where she lived … she was absolutely in the right place. You should be able to walk on the pavement without this happening.'

Finally, after three weeks, there was a breakthrough and an arrest. 'I think it was about four o'clock in the morning when Detective Kennedy phoned to say that they had some good news and they came to the house,' Grace remembered. 'They'd been working very hard on the case and they said, "We've apprehended three, there are still two more."'

'We thought it might have been two people responsible because one had to be driving the car. The final figure of five was monstrous,' says Garry.

'I went through everything I felt Anita had gone through,' Grace says slowly. 'That was with me for a long time. I did feel some anger. You feel, "How could another human being treat someone in such a way?"'

The Lynches had never heard of the men involved. They were simply names. The Lynch family came face to face with the men at the committal hearing at Westmead, and later at Glebe. Garry later admitted that he was afraid of making close contact with any of the men responsible for the murder.

'I felt I'd rip them to bits with my bare hands. People thought we managed to hold onto our dignity but within me there was a raging tide.'

Standing before them at Westmead were 'five ordinary hoons', as Garry described them. 'I thought at the time, "You dumb witless fools, you don't even realise what you've done.

'I looked at them … and they were very cowed … not coward but "cowed". Their heads were hung, they looked as if they were ashamed … well they could have been because I don't suppose I was a great sight to see for them … but, we went through it, got that over … and they just took them back to their holding cells and we waited for the next move, which was the court case.'

Michael Murdoch's mother also asked if she could speak to the Lynches outside the court. 'She couldn't believe her son had been involved,' Grace says. 'She was a mother, you know … she said he wasn't a violent boy, she thought he had just got in with the wrong group.'

The Lynches were left alone to deal with the death of their beautiful daughter for a full year before the trial started in March 1987. The kindness of strangers – letters, flowers, prayers, even gifts – and the sympathy and support of family and friends helped them enormously. For a time, Garry Lynch carried hate in his heart but he worried that he would become like the men who murdered his daughter.

'We felt we had to attend the trial to represent Anita and to see justice was done,' said Grace. 'We were supported by our good friend Anne King who came to the court every day for the three months that the trial lasted.

'Friends told us we'd be very hurt but I couldn't have been hurt any more … It was very harrowing but it was something we had to do … otherwise Anita would have just been another murder victim. And we cared, and we wanted to know the details of what had happened to her, so it was very hard.'

The trial was 'gruelling' for the Lynch family and Anita's close circle of friends – graphic photos, clinical evidence presented of what happened to her on the night she died and endless legal discussions about what the jury could and couldn't see. There was an intense argument to prove that Anita had been conscious to the very end. She had fought for her life, putting up her hand to stop the blade in Travers' hand from cutting her throat.

When the trial got bogged down in points of law, Grace became indignant. 'That's our daughter … that's Anita,' Grace thought. 'It was almost unbelievable.'

The jury returned its verdict on 10 June 1987. 'They cheered and clapped,' Garry remembered. '[And] they threw it all at us … directly, you could feel it. My immediate reaction was, "Thank God … the pages are going to close and that will be it."'

The Lynches were not there for the final sentencing. Garry says, 'When I heard the sentence, it was almost terrifyingly satisfying on my part. "Never to be released". I don't want anybody to let us down on that. It was up to the court and the gaol to enforce it.'

After the trial, Garry told the media, 'Now I want you all to hear this – I believe we've given you a pretty fair go. Now we want you to step back and give us a go. Give us a break, OK?' But the trial was not the end of the ordeal. All five men appealed the severity of their sentences, although Travers would withdraw his appeal. Three of the applicants had their appeals dismissed, but Les Murphy would be granted a retrial in July 1990.

On 8 July 1990, the Lynches found themselves back at Darlinghurst Supreme Court where Les Murphy was found guilty once again. Although they had been through so much, Garry and Grace still found the capacity to reach out and forgive. The father of the Murphy boys worked at Blacktown RSL, which Garry Lynch frequented. After the trial, he made an effort to seek out Mr Murphy and shake his hand, telling him he did not hold him responsible for what his sons had done.

Garry and Grace remained in the same weatherboard house in Sullivan Street, Blacktown. Garry pursued spiritualism, even spending time in an Indian ashram, and travelled around Australia with his family. He suffered a stroke after the trial, but he willed himself to recover. The couple drew their remaining daughter closer, realising that Kathryn had lost 'her best friend' and they supported her through a marriage breakdown just as they had Anita.

The Lynches had to come to terms with such a senseless crime and the loss of a precious life. 'I think of her every day,' Grace later said, 'not as a murdered person [but] how she was and how she is now. She's at peace.'

At the core of the Christian faith, Christians turn death into a positive experience. The Lynches lobbied the government for 'truth in sentencing' laws, which came into being in 1990 and helped set up the Homicide Victims Support Group. 'If we didn't have faith, I just don't know how we could have coped,' Grace later said. 'I often wonder how people manage without it.'

'It was a tragedy that you think could not happen to anyone, until it happened to you,' Garry later wrote. 'It's impossible to realise what surviving members of the family endure. We were totally shocked and devastated but knew that we had to remain strong to cope with the police investigation, media and later the court procedures and rituals.

But it was also Anita's memory that got them through. 'She'd be saying, "You must, you must go on with your lives" and we had help from friends and even strangers,' says Grace. 'I think if bitterness comes into it, it affects you and it affects your health and I know Anita, she'd be saying, "Don't be bitter." We did that for her sake.'

Garry explained, 'You see, what you have to understand is we've lost a beautiful, loving daughter – we've lost her physical being, but we've been recompensed with a wonderful uplifting, supportive, spiritual being.' He found quiet ways to communicate with his daughter … meditation, prayer, writing to her, dreaming of her.

But the pain was still there. 'At times there is even agony,' he admitted 20 years after the crime. 'It's only brief, but it hits you and, oh boy…it's like a rapier going through your heart but you know it's going to come. You can't avoid it and you've got to just brace yourself. It's a long and jagged and searing hurt but it doesn't kill you.'

'…and out of it,' Grace added, 'you become a stronger person.'

Anita Cobby … attractive, vivacious and full of life, as snapped by a city photographer in Sydney's Martin Place shortly before her murder.

(Above and opposite) Constable Debbie Wallace, dressed as Anita Cobby, conducts a re-enactment of the young nurse's final walk through Blacktown a week after her body was found in a Prospect paddock, 9 February 1986.

Anita Cobby as her family and friends remember her … young, vibrant, happy.

(Above) Accused murderer Michael Murdoch, centre in handcuffs, shows detectives Ian Kennedy (left) and Hugh Dundas the spot where Anita Cobby was abducted on Newton Road on the night of 2 February 1986.

(Right) Murdoch with detectives at the bottom of Reen Road, Prospect, where nurse Anita Cobby was dragged over a barbed wire fence, raped and then murdered.

The diminutive Les Murphy shows detectives Paul Raue (left), Garry Heskett (second left) and Tony Waters (right) where Anita Cobby's clothing was disposed of in a fire in the backyard of John Travers' Doonside home.

Les Murphy with detectives in the back yard of Travers' home where he lived with Lisa Travers in a caravan.

Les Murphy shows detectives when he and four others took Anita Cobby on the night she was raped and murdered. The 'boiler paddock' on Reen Road was a desolate and barren place.

(Above) Gary Murphy shows detectives Graham Rosetta (left) and Tony Waters (right) the direction from which the five men dragged Anita Cobby through the paddock in Reen Road. Note the mark on Murphy's face which was caused during his capture the previous night.

(Left) Gary Murphy stands at the spot Anita Cobby's body was found. Note the cows in the background paddock.

After he was captured, Mick Murphy was taken through on a crime scene 'run-around' by detectives Ian Kennedy (left) and Paul Raue (back to camera). Murphy is pictured in Newton Road, Blacktown, where the abduction of Anita Cobby took place.

Mick Murphy on Reed Road, showing the point where Anita Cobby was taken through the barbed wire fence and to her death. Note the throng of media at the police barricade at the top of the road.

John Travers (left) in handcuffs after being allowed to attend the funeral of his mother in 1989 'on compassionate grounds'. Travers was only 18 year old when he murdered Anita Cobby and will undoubtedly spend the rest of his life in prison. (Courtesy Newspix)

Gary Murphy, the youngest of three Murphy brothers found guilty of the abduction, rape and murder of Anita Cobby. The Murphy brothers were petty criminals with long rap sheets before they were arrested for the abduction, rape and murder of Anita Cobby in 1987.

Angry mob yells: 'Hang the dirty bastards'

Three charged over Cobby murder

A MOB shouted "hang the bastards" and strung a noose from a nearby building as three men charged with the murder of Sydney nurse Anita Cobby were led from Blacktown Court yesterday.

By TRACEY ARTHUR

The three – Michael James Murdoch, 18, of Westmead, John Raymond Travers, 18, of Doonside and Leslie Joseph Murphy, 22, also of Doonside – were arrested in police raids yesterday morning and during the weekend.

The badly-battered and naked body of pretty Ms Cobby, 26, was found in a paddock by a local farmer in Reen Rd, Prospect, on February 2.

The accused men were booed yesterday on their way into court, where they appeared before Magistrate Mr Ross McDermid.

Guard

Police tightened security in and around the court while a guard of 10 detectives surrounded the three men in court.

Police were also called in to control the mob of about 200 people as they crowded around the police station and court for three hours calling for the return of capital punishment.

Many of the people were yelling "hang the dirty [illegible] suffer" "we want to see their faces – they don't deserve protection".

The three men have each been charged with murder, inflicting grievous bodily harm with intent to have sexual intercourse and kidnap.

Murdoch is also charged with assault and robbery.

Murphy is also charged with receiving stolen goods worth $1000 and Travers is on other unrelated charges of assault and committing an act of in[illegible].

The [illegible] were remanded in custody and will appear in Westmead Coroner's Court [illegible] Thursday.

[illegible] will also appear [illegible] Blacktown Court on March [illegible].

The arrests of the three men were the result of intense police investigations and public response.

Police yesterday took the men to Newton Rd, Blacktown, where it is alleged Ms Cobby was kidnapped and then on to the paddock where her body was found.

The three men are in [illegible]

Michael Patrick Murphy . . . wanted

Garry Stephen Murphy . . . wanted

Police seek two brothers for questioning

POLICE last night were hunting two brothers for questioning over the murder of Anita Cobby.

Michael Patrick Murphy, 33, and Garry Stephen Murphy, 2[illegible], are brothers of Leslie Joseph Murphy, 22, one of the three charged with Anita's murder and remanded in custody.

Michael Murphy, believed to be [illegible] has twice escaped from jail.

He was serving cumulative sentences totalling 24 years – in a low-security prison – for armed robberies, burglary and escaping.

He last escaped from Silverwater Jail on December 27 last year.

Police swooped on a house in the Riverstone area near Blacktown [illegible] minutes but they seized a knife with an 18cm long blade.

They also recovered a quantity of clothing which was being examined by forensic experts last night.

Two men were seen driving at high speed from the house just as police cars sped to the area yesterday.

Police were searching for a [illegible] 1974 Ford Cortina with the regis[illegible]

Wanted man on the run

By DENNIS RINGROSE

ONE of the two men still wanted for questioning over the murder of Anita Cobby has twice escaped from prison and earlier faced charges of attempting to escape from jail.

Michael Patrick Murphy, 33, is on the run following his escape from Silverwater Jail on December 27 last year.

He had been serving cumulative sentences totalling 24 years for a lengthy series of crimes involving robbery and break, enter and steal.

State Government officials yesterday admitted he had been given a low security C2 rating after expert assessment.

Property

Murphy was working in a prison industry, the Silverwater light engineering factory.

"His history is one mainly involving property offences," said a spokesman for the Corrective Services Minister, Mr Akister.

Murphy was first [illegible] sentenced to 18 months jail in early 1972 for car stealing with a six-month non-parole period.

Later that year he was sentenced to 12[illegible] years jail on charges of robbery and break, enter [illegible]

Raging! THE WEEK'S TOP GIGS

Daily Mirror

Thursday, February 27, 1986

ANITA: NURSES HANG DUMMY AT COURT

Big protest as suspects face coroner

NOOSE: The dummy hung by protesters outside Westmead Coroner's Court today

JEERS of "hang them" and "gas the bastards" and a dummy hanging from a noose greeted the men accused of murdering beauty queen Anita Cobby today.

Michael and Garry Murphy, captured in a dramatic raid at Glenfield late last night, were met by an angry crowd of 300 at Blacktown court.

One placard read "Kill the animals or they'll do it again."

On a building site adjacent to the Petty Sessions courthouse workmen again draped a noose from the roof.

And at Westmead Coroner's Court a crowd of more than 100 nurses and hospital staff hung a wire dummy dressed in overalls from a noose.

The crowd bayed its approval. A sign saying "Give Anita's killers a free operation (without anaesthetic)" was put under the court sign while the dummy swung in the background.

Another noose was swinging from a street light nearby.

Nurses from Westmead Hospital bashed on police vehicles as they ferried three of the men into the

● Continued page 2

LATE FINAL EXTRA ● No 13,[illegible] ● PHONE [illegible] ● TV P 26 ● FINANCE P 40 ● WEATHER [illegible]

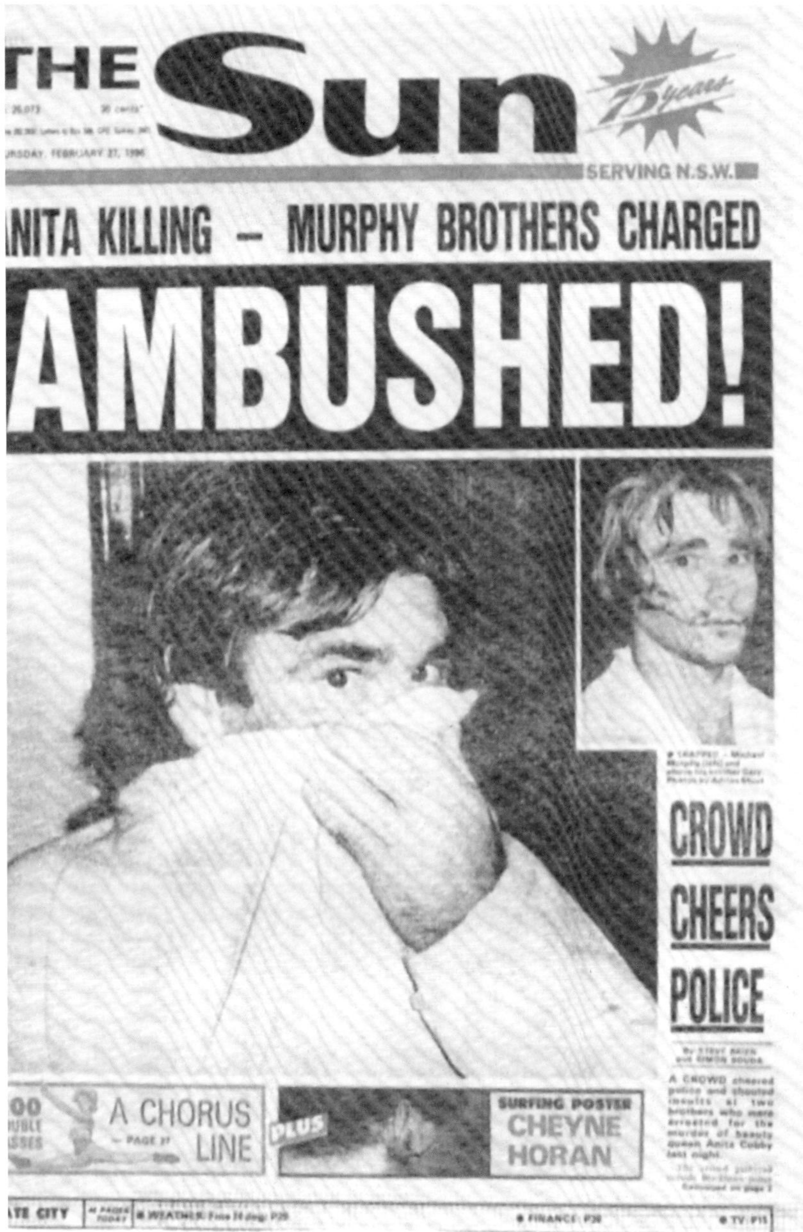

THE Sun

75 years

SERVING N.S.W.

NITA KILLING – MURPHY BROTHERS CHARGED

AMBUSHED!

CROWD CHEERS POLICE

A CROWD cheered police and shouted insults at two brothers who were arrested for the murder of beauty queen Anita Cobby last night.

A CHORUS LINE

PLUS

SURFING POSTER CHEYNE HORAN

TV P11

The sensational reporting of the Anita Cobby Case dominated the Sydney newspapers in the early months of 1986.

Part of the crowd milling outside Blacktown Police Station when the men responsible for the abduction, rape and murder of Anita Cobby were arrested, 24 February 1986.

A suspect in the Anita Cobby murder covers his face as he is driven to the cells at Blacktown in front of the media and an angry crowed. (Courtesy Newspix)

Garry and Grace 'Peg' Lynch address the media after the five men who murdered their daughter were found guilty in June 1987. No parents placed in such a position could have acted with more courage, compassion and Christian forgiveness. (Courtesy Newspix)

In the years immediately after the death of his daughter, Garry Lynch and his wife devoted their lives to helping others struggling with the trauma of vicious crime through their involvement with the Homicide Victims Support Group. (Courtesy Newspix)

ANITA
COBBY
RESERVE

Kathryn Szyszka, the sister of Anita Cobby, and her daughter Olivia at the naming of a reserve in Sullivan Street, Blacktown, in Anita's honour. On the 29th anniversary of Anita's death, her family were joined (background, from left) by former Chief Inspector Garry Raymond, Detective Sergeant Garry Mereweather and Constable Genelle Warne. (Courtesy Newspix).

Anita Cobby's final resting place at Pinegrove Memorial Park, Minchinbury, in Western Sydney. Thirty years after her death, family, friends and complete strangers leave flowers, cards and even gifts at her gravesite in her memory. (Photo Alan J. Whiticker)

All pictures courtesy NSW Police, except where otherwise noted.

IAN KENNEDY REMEMBERS

By his own admission, Ian Kennedy is an 'Eastern Suburbs boy.' Nicknamed 'Speed' as a young rugby player because of his lack of speed … 'I should have been called 'speedless' he laughs … the Sydney Boys High student was 'a little fat hooker' in third grade, with future internationals Phil Smith and John Brass the star centres in firsts. 'I made a break at training and Phil Smith ran up beside me going half pace and said, "Go Speed go!" It just stuck.'

'Speed' Kennedy played more than 200 games for Randwick during the late 1960s and 1970s and won five premierships with the club, which included the Ella Brothers in 1978–79. 'I used to run with [league legend] Ron Coote, who was my next door neighbour at Maroubra.' Kennedy had offers to go to the professional game in the early 1970s, but resisted the urge. 'I played rugby league for the police until 1973, but Randwick was going on a European tour and I wanted to go on that, so I stuck with the amateur game.'

Kennedy is also a fourth generation police officer. 'My uncle, grandfather and great grandfather all served with the police. Dad was in the army during World War II and when he tried to join on his return, he was knocked back with flat feet. "I just spent four years in the infantry and now you tell me I have flat feet!" he told them.'

In February 1986, Kennedy was a Senior Detective Sergeant with the Homicide Squad in Sydney when he was asked to take charge of the Anita Cobby murder investigation.

'The Anita Cobby case is in the most shocking category,' he says. 'The mere size of the knife used puts it there. We found a knife at John Travers' place, which was not the murder weapon … 9 inches with a serrated edge … a knife he cut the throat of a sheep with. We also bought a knife similar to this from a local hunting store because they told us they had sold Travers a similar knife sometime before the murder.'

'It's a knife that you would use for no other purpose except hunting … it was too big of a knife for even scaling and gutting a fish. To think that's the type of weapon that killed Anita is shocking.'

'As a policeman, I would rather have a fight with someone with a gun than with a knife … they can miss with a gun or the bullet can go straight through you, but if they slice you with a knife, it can rip and tear and do a lot more damage.'

'You can see the reasons why Judge Maxwell said, "I will show you the same mercy" in sentencing all five to life.'

Despite his years on the force, Kennedy found the case difficult, both professionally and personally. 'I'd leave home every morning around 6.00 o'clock and take an hour and a half to get to Blacktown every morning and an hour and half home,' he recalls. 'I remember being pulled over by the highway patrol because I had mud all over the back numberplate. I hadn't had much sleep for a couple of days at that stage and I was getting pretty cranky about it ...

The worst time in the murder for me was when we got the first offenders and we went around to the Lynch home around 5.30 in the morning. I rang them up, "Grace, put the kettle on – I'm coming around with Detective Inspector Pat Toohey," A wonderful Irishman based at Blacktown, an old football player and an immaculately dressed man, Pat had witnessed one of the interviews with Murdoch. The Lynches opened the door and Pat pointed at me and said, "Have a look at this man. He hasn't slept for three days ..."

'I told them, "I have some news for you ... we just arrested three for the murder and there's another two we're looking for." Garry replied, "There are five of them?" I could see the shock on their faces. That was the worst time for me. At that moment, they knew what had happened to their daughter.'

'Before I went in there, I thought about what I was going to say but I thought honesty was the best policy ... it was worse than delivering a death message. In that situation, you don't know the people but by this time we had got to know the Lynches so well. They knew us and were depending on us and were so close to us and here I was. I was building up their expectation that it was over and it wasn't. I didn't want to let them down and I felt we had by not having it all resolved. I thought what a terrible thing to have to tell anyone ... I was giving them worse news than they had just got.'

'Unfortunately, we are the deliverers of bad news. That's part of the job. The worst part was seeing a beautiful young girl on the table and the extent of her injuries during the post mortem.'

'We broadcast that we were looking for the last two suspects and information came in that Mick and Gary Murphy were at a flat in Glenfield. There was a protocol about forced entry, who went left and who went right. We knocked the door down and I was first in with a shotgun. Mick Murphy was sitting on the lounge with a child on his lap. The look on his face, I think he thought he was going to get shot ...'

'I ordered him to lie on the floor and he put the child to one side and he did what I asked. I immediately put my foot on his head ... the reason I did that was I wanted to be sure he didn't have a concealed gun, and with other police running through the house checking the bedrooms, and Gary Murphy running into the backyard, it wasn't as if I could search him one handed and put the gun on the ground, so I stood on his head and patted him down where I could while balancing the gun in one hand. It immobilised him.'

That protocol was to be put under scrutiny during the committal hearing and trial.

'When Mick Murphy's barrister later asked me in the Coroner's Court if I knew how he got some marks on his face, I am sure they were expecting me to say, "No, I have no idea" but instead I told them, "Probably mat burn from me standing on his head."

'"Why would you do that?" he asked and I explained my reasoning. The detective senior sergeant who witnessed Murphy's record of interview when we were back in the station asked Murphy if he had any complaints about the way the interview was conducted and Murphy said no.

During the committal hearing, Travers' barrister asked the detective senior sergeant if he saw any marks on Mick Murphy's face. 'Yes,' he said, 'from mat burn'.

Kennedy takes up the story: 'The barrister replied, "Oh, mat burn! And I suppose you're an expert?" The other said, "Actually I'm the police light heavyweight wrestling champion and I have been for the last nine years and I know what mat burn looks like." I didn't know this. I only met him the night I came in with Murphy in custody.

'That barrister couldn't take a trick. He was expecting the cops to deny this ... the reason we said this was because that's exactly how it happened. Gary Murphy got tackled into a fence running outside and pissed himself. He also ended up with a mark on his face.'

As leader of the task force, Kennedy said it was essential that all arrests and interviews be conducted professionally. 'When we had a briefing about where we were going and what we were to do, I said to the team, "We're all full of emotion because we're getting close to catching these blokes so it's crucial how we handle it. Everyone's tired but we need to remain professional ... if we arrest them and belt them, and they complain, the jury might let them off because of what happened. And then I have to go to Mr Lynch and tell him "we got the right blokes but they got off" and he'll say "all because you couldn't keep your hands to yourself" and I don't want that to happen …

'We were the Homicide Squad, the best of the best, that's how people viewed us … there is nothing more serious in our criminal code than a homicide. We had to set the right example and we didn't want officers following a bad example. We wanted a result, a conviction, and we didn't want to lose because we used unnecessary force.

'We didn't touch them when we got them back to the station. During the trial, Mick Murphy said he was belted. When they asked him who did it, he said he didn't know which one. The Crown prosecutor Allan Saunders paraded the cops through the court and he couldn't identify one. The jury knew it was bullshit.'

'I was proud that the team obeyed those instructions. Every investigation is a training for someone,' he says. 'It's an easy example to set when you worked with detectives like Garry Heskett and Kevin Raue before, and although I didn't know the Blacktown guys, Garry and Kevin did, so they picked a team that could work together. The blokes we had were great.'

Kennedy, however, has little to say for the five men they arrested. 'They wanted to blame everyone else but themselves. Gary Murphy said he wasn't even there. It was laughable … they weren't the brightest tools in the shed but very street smart.

'They were smartarses, all of them. They were all smiling, laughing in court.'

Asked to explain why they acted like that when their futures were on the line, Kennedy says one word. 'Contempt … contempt for the court, the police, the system, society and the victim. They showed no mercy or sympathy.

'When we were interviewing them about the stolen car, and later the murder, we could tell they were lying. We asked Murdoch, "Where were you on the night of the murder?" "I was home watching TV," he said. "What was on?" "Don't know." You could tell from his body language he was lying. He was so nervous.

'Mick Murphy was the more experienced crook; I can't say he was the leader, but having been in gaol, they probably listened to what he said because that's the way they grew up … they looked up to him.'

'Travers was wild. We knew from the background information given to us that he was a nasty bloke. We knew that the nature of his sexual assault on the young man in Western Australia, where he pulled the hair back and held a knife to his throat while having sex, was a mirror of the Cobby murder.'

'Travers was at another level in brutality,' Kennedy says. 'He was an animal, taking a sheep to a party and having sex with it and cutting its throat in front of people. It says a lot about his upbringing, the lack of role models he had. He was deprived of a lot of things, I suppose, including parental control and a good education.'

After the case was finished, there was a release. 'The public demonstrations at Blacktown Court and the emotion at the end of the trial, the only other public show of emotion that rivals the Cobby case in my memory is the recent outpouring of sympathy for the victims of the Lindt Café siege in December 2014.

'I can't say what was going through their minds, whether they finally realised the public was against them ... and these [protestors] were people who didn't even know Anita Cobby. They were absolutely appalled at what they did to her, that they did it in their backyard and the locals were very protective of their community.

'We went to the pub and people were buying us drinks ... walking past and saying, "Well done, boys". Cops are good at having a beer after an arrest, but publicans were inviting us to go to their pubs. We didn't knock them back too many times other than the fact that they needed to let us know that not everyone in the Western Suburbs were like these animals.'

'I don't know if you're ever completely satisfied as an investigating detective because you can never bring the murder victim back to life. All you can do is say, "A job well done, boys ... we've done our best and the people responsible have been brought to justice." Whether the family have some sort of closure, it's hard to say, but at least we've given them a chance to get on with their lives knowing justice has been done. It was very satisfying.'

'In saying that, I think we all got a shock with the sentence ... not the usual 'life' sentence, but for the rest of their lives. Les Murphy got a retrial because of his low IQ and he got convicted to life, but the judge did not say for the rest of his natural life, so he may get out.'

There are also the personal costs, Kennedy says. 'The people who suffer the most when you are investigating a crime is your wife and kids ... you're working often 40 days straight. Every day, travelling to and from work, all I'm thinking about is the case. I was totally devoted to that and ignoring the ones who love me most ... its takes over your day to day existence and it makes you very selfish to be able to focus on it.'

At the end of the investigation, Kennedy was heartened when the task force received two cards signed by almost every police cadet from Goulburn Police Academy, saying "congratulations". 'When you get something like that from your own … my own satisfaction was that they felt good about taking part in the investigation. They were part of it and they felt that they had contributed in some small way, although we didn't find anything there … they would have remembered that experience the remainder of their careers.'

CHAPTER TWELVE

THE LAW

'There seems to be a fashion, among some in the criminal justice system, for a kind of misplaced altruism, that it is somehow a noble thing to assist a criminal to evade conviction ... Justice is not achieved by ambush, trickery, dragging proceedings out in a war of attrition with witnesses.'

Deputy Senior Crown Prosecutor Margaret Cunneen, Sir Ninian Stephen Lecture, 2005

On 25 June 1987, Raymond John Paterson, 35, of Tivoli Place, Doonside, was found guilty of being an accessory to murder after the fact. The jury found him guilty of two counts after deliberating for more than nine hours and being locked up overnight. Later, Paterson said he did not know they had killed the girl and that the culprits had stayed with him not on Monday, but Tuesday, 4 February so as not to incriminate himself. He changed his story and gave up names because he thought that was what the police wanted to hear and for his trouble, he was sentenced to eight years gaol. He would serve eight months.

The following day, the trial of the two women charged with harbouring the Murphy brothers at Glenfield commenced. Both pleaded not guilty. Debra McAskill was acquitted. 'I was satisfied,' said Justice Maxwell, 'that afterwards both were frightened and at a loss as to what to do' and that McAskill wanted them out of the flat, even though they did not contact police. Mavis Saunders was described as a 'simple person', 'floundering' and 'out of her depth'. She was placed on a $1000 bond.

Following the trial, the new Labor Premier Barry Unsworth made a public commitment on behalf of his Government that the five men who were found guilty would never be on the streets again. On 28 September 1988, however, Central Criminal Court was informed that Travers would appeal against his life sentence and the recommendation from the trial judge, Justice Maxwell, that he never be released.

On 10 November 1987, Ms Robin Donnelly, barrister for Travers, said her client would withdraw his appeal. The teenaged killer had obviously been given legal advice that there were no grounds where an appeal would be possibly upheld, but detective Kevin Raue later offered an interesting insight into Travers' possible motives. 'He was the only one to plead guilty ... perhaps he wanted spare his family any more pain.'

On 7 December 1988, appeals by Michael Murdoch and Mick, Gary and Les Murphy were dismissed by the NSW Supreme Court. All except Mick Murphy, however, were granted special leave to appeal to the High Court of Australia. The following year, on 30 May 1989, Michael Murdoch and Gary Murphy had their appeals dismissed by the High Court. Les Murphy, however, had his sentence quashed and he was granted a new trial in July 1990.

There were four grounds for the appeal that were common to all applicants. The first arose from media publicity at the time of the trial in March 1987 in which Mick Murphy was identified as an escaped prisoner by *The Sun* newspaper and the subsequent refusal of Justice Maxwell to postpone the trial for another six months.

It was the view of the High Court that Justice Maxwell had not erred in postponing the trial: 'It is fundamental that, for an accused to have a fair trial, the jury should reach its verdict by reference only to the evidence admitted at trial and not by reference to facts or alleged facts gathered from the media or some outside source. However, the might of media publicity in "sensational" cases makes such a pristine approach virtually impossible.'

As Justice Maxwell observed back in 1987, the Anita Cobby case would continue to attract great publicity, no matter when the trial was heard.

The importance of a fair trial for the accused is essential, but it is not the only consideration a judge has to balance. It is important that anyone charged with a criminal offence be brought to trial as quickly as possible. Not only is it in his or her own interest, but it is in the interest of witnesses and the family of the victim as well.

Trials should not be adjourned unnecessarily, the Court maintained, otherwise the justice system would be clogged up for years and years on end.

The second ground of appeal alleged that Justice Maxwell should have allowed counsel for the accused to challenge a juror 'for cause' to be dismissed from the jury. The potential juror had asked to be excused, saying, 'I can't give these people a fair trial.'

It was not told whether this incident happened in the first trial or second trial, but Justice Maxwell's refusal to allow a challenge was sustained because the 'necessary foundation for a challenge could not be laid.' The High Court stated: 'We consider that his decision and the manner in which he implemented it by giving suitable directions to the jury were the appropriate steps to take in all the circumstances.'

The third ground for appeal centred on Justice Maxwell's refusal to allow counsel for the accused to investigate the basis on which a warrant was issued to fit a listening device to Miss X. It wasn't that the warrant failed to authorise what Miss X had done, but that counsel for the accused wanted to investigate whether there was a 'procedural or substantive error' in relation to its issue.

The High Court dismissed this appeal because the warrant to fit the listening device was granted by a judge of the Supreme Court and thus, being an order of a superior court, its validity was to be presumed. The admissibility of Miss X's evidence depended on the existence of the warrant and there was no challenge to the jurisdiction of the Supreme Court to grant the warrant.

The fourth and final ground for appeal advanced by all the applicants was regarding a remark made by Justice Maxwell in response to the assertion by counsel for the accused that statements presented as evidence by police were 'a complete fake' and that the accused had been 'victims of violence' by the police officers. Maxwell had instructed the jury:

'It hardly needs me to say that these allegations constitute grave allegations against the police officers concerned. You are entitled to have regard to the whole of the surrounding relevant evidence of any submission put to you by any counsel. If one were, for example, to include those unidentified detectives, two at a time, three times, who visited Michael Patrick Murphy in the interview room and assaulted him in the absence of the officers taking the record of interview, there would appear to be some 26 officers involved in these conspiracies, assaults and fabrications. I am not again intending to be entering the fact-finding arena which is your arena not mine, but not that it proves conclusively one way or the other, but on the probabilities, on what is likely to be the situation, and I am not talking about the onus of proof, what is the likelihood? Is it that you get 26 police officers? It is a matter for you.'

In court, no one applicant challenged the 26 police officers involved in the case. It was up to the jury to decide between the likelihood of the police 'entering into a conspiracy' or the Crown proving their case 'beyond a reasonable doubt.' The jury believed the police and the High Court upheld Justice Maxwell's ruling. Interestingly, at Blacktown Police Station when Mick Murphy asserted that he had been bashed, the Inspector in charge of the station asked him 'which one' and brought all the officers in one-by-one. Murphy said he 'couldn't remember'.

There remained three grounds of appeal, however, for individual applicants. Complaints relating to only Gary Murphy and Michael Murdoch were dismissed, but the third was that Justice Maxwell was in error when he refused to allow professional evidence that proved Les Murphy was of 'limited intellectual capacity' and that 'the confessional material adduced through the police record of interview with him was thereby rendered inadmissible or at any rate dangerously unreliable.'

The Court of Criminal Appeal regarded the matter as 'finely balanced' but the three-judge bench ruled on majority that Les Murphy's conviction would be quashed and he should be granted a retrial. The particular psychologist called by lawyers to refute that Murphy's confession was in his own words was denied by Justice Maxwell. The judge doubted the psychologist had a background in literacy and thus he could not have provided 'admissible expert evidence' about the wording used.

The High Court, however, ruled that Murphy may not have fully understood certain questions put to him and, in framing his answers, he may have used various words and expressions not in his vocabulary such as 'unconscious', 'intercourse', 'penis', 'vagina' and 'incident'.

At his retrial in July 1990, however, Les Murphy was found to be 'functioning intellectually' when he gave the police his statement. He may not have been able to read the statement because he opted to have a detective read it to him before signing it, but it was determined he understood what the words meant in the context of the statement. The Crown was also able to prove that Murphy had used certain words before when they tabled a previous signed statement made by Murphy when he was charged with assaulting a 14-year-old girl in Sydney's Hyde Park in 1982.

Sentenced to life for a second time, the retrial judge Justice Jeremy Badgery-Parker declined to send Murphy to gaol for the length of his natural life. He believed this sentence gave Murphy 'some hope for the future' and an incentive to rehabilitate.

* * *

On 22 May 1987, the *Daily Telegraph* reported Mr Athol Moffit, QC, the retired president of the NSW Court of Appeal, as saying that 'the criminal trial system is too heavily tilted in favour of the accused, and the access to legal aid meant that many were not pleading guilty because they thought they had a chance to manipulate the system … '

This was especially true of the trial of the five men charge with the murder of Anita Cobby and associated offences. The Lynch family, having been centred at the eye of the legal hurricane spinning around them, could not believe the judicial battle raging in front of them. Garry Lynch later wrote:

'Despite the solemnity of the proceedings, the atmosphere was nothing short of absurd. The ceremony, the black gown and unkempt wigs of all the attendants, the thespian ways of the defence counsel rambling on with endless discussions on points of law, seeing everything as "prejudicial to my client" trying to make a case when there was no case, particularly against the police, made it all seem a monstrous manipulation of words and time … there was constant sniping between the prosecutor and the defence counsel. Even Justice Maxwell in his summing up at the end of the trial said he had never heard such vitriolic exchanges in his 40 years before the bench.'

When defence lawyers hitch their reputations and careers to accused rapists and murderers of defenceless women and take on the testimony and good names of investigating detectives, then the result is always going to be ugly.

Lawyer Leigh Johnson agrees the atmosphere of the trial was 'hostile'. Johnson and lawyer Sandy Wetmore first met with Gary Murphy at Parklea Gaol when he was awaiting trial. By their own admission, their initial conversation with Gary Murphy was 'all over the place.' 'He's not educated to a very high standard and told a convoluted story about stealing a car and changing the number plates,' recalls Johnson. When the subject turned to rape and murder, he simply said, "I weren't there."'

Johnson didn't believe him at first. At the time, Gary Murphy couldn't remember where he was on the night of the murder (he later produced an alibi that he was with a girl) and he had signed a statement. But when Murphy and the three other defendants told their respective counsel that their confessions had been 'fabricated' by detectives and their signatures 'bashed' out of them, the lawyers had a defence.

Johnson said her client had 'little experience or capacity to instruct his solicitor' and she launched appeals on his behalf all the way to the High Court of Australia, all of which were ultimately unsuccessful. She maintains that her client was innocent, it was a 'trial by media' and even if there were a retrial, the Murphy brothers would not have got a fair hearing. Johnson didn't escape without personal criticism either. The controversial lawyer was pilloried in the media and in legal circles for forming a close relationship with convicted murderers, for 'pitying' her client and for crying when Gary Murphy was found guilty.

The Lynch family showed compassion towards the defence lawyers charged with defending the five men. 'Somebody has to do it,' Garry said. 'They may be reluctant to do it, but give them the credit that they have been asked to do this ... and that will be a terrible thing they have to do.'

What angered Garry and Grace Lynch, however, was that at the end of the trial the four accused men were allowed to make unsworn, uncross-examinable statements from the dock.

'Of course, these statements contradicted their statements to the police where each of them had accused each other of rape,' Lynch later wrote. '... I saw it as a monstrous travesty of justice. In 1994, we managed to get the NSW Attorney General John Hannaford to change the law of allowing unsworn and uncross-examinable statements from the dock.'

The Anita Cobby case challenged and ultimately changed the law. A petition to reintroduce the death penalty for Anita Cobby's murderers privately initiated by a public servant attracted 20,000 signatures in six weeks. While the debate raged there were times, Garry Lynch later admitted, when he could have 'quite happily become the executioner.'

'We stayed absolutely clear of that,' Garry remarked. 'We gave no support to any ideas that people had for this to be re-enacted ... so gradually that all died down, just faded out.'

Murder committed in NSW before 1990 carried a 'life' sentence but, in reality, this punishment did not mean for natural life. Penal servitude for life was substituted as the mandatory penalty for murder in New South Wales following the abolition of the death penalty in 1955. It rarely meant that a person would stay in custody for the rest of his or her natural life. Rather, it was an indeterminate sentence subject to review at a time deemed appropriate by the executive. By the end of the 1970s, the large majority of prisoners serving life sentences for the crime of murder could expect to be released within 15–20 years.

In 1990, the year that the average 'life' sentence served was just 15 years, the NSW State Liberal Government under Nick Greiner's leadership adopted 'truth in sentencing' legislation that changed the law so that a life sentence meant for the term of natural life. Ten prisoners who committed heinous murders before 1990 had their papers marked 'NTBR' (never to be released) – Allan Baker and Kevin Crump, convicted for the 1973 murder of Ian Lamb and conspiracy to murder Virginia Morse in Queensland; John Travers, Michael Murdoch and Gary, Les and Mick Murphy, convicted in 1986 for the murder of Anita Cobby; and Matthew Elliott, Bronson Blessington and Stephen 'Shorty' Jamieson, the murderers of Janine Balding in 1988.

In 1997, Bob Carr's Labor Government passed a law that these ten men must serve 20 years before applying for a review of their life sentences. With Baker and Crump the first to apply for a redetermination of their sentences, the NSW Parliament passed a further law in 2001 that these ten must serve 30 years before applying for parole and that none of the ten can be released on parole until they are 'in imminent danger of dying' or are so incapacitated that they do not have 'the physical ability to do harm to any person'.

In the words of then NSW Premier Bob Carr, the ten were effectively 'cemented into their cells' for the rest of their natural lives with no hope for parole.

'Truth in sentencing' provides a more transparent sentencing system whereby sentences imposed actually match sentences served by offenders. It has also made for a much harsher sentencing system in NSW with a significant increase in the average periods served in custody across a broad range of offences, including murder.

However, the indeterminate nature of a life sentence has been the subject of criticism by penologists, psychologists and those concerned with the gaol system and the punishment of offenders generally. A NSW Supreme Court judgement in 1991 noted: 'Such a sentence deprives a prisoner of any fixed goal to aim for, it robs him of any incentive and it is personally destructive of his morale. The life sentence imposes intolerable burdens upon most prisoners because of their incarceration for an indeterminate period, and the result of that imposition has been an increased difficulty in their management by the gaol authorities.'

The Anita Cobby killers were to experience that reality first hand.

CHAPTER THIRTEEN

The Murphys

'They were all different in their personalities and demeanour... Les was intimidating and spoke aggressively. (He) was the smallest of the Murphy brothers and he had a real hard edge to him. Michael and Gary were a little more subdued and remorseful, but believed they should not have been gaoled for the crime ...'

Journalist, Julia Sheppard

Dulcie and Leslie Murphy raised nine children, seven boys and two girls, in the tough, inner-city suburbs of Glebe, Rozelle and Erskineville. Father Les worked at the old Tooheys Brewery near Central Railway Station and spent his weekends operating a small fishing trawler. Mother Dulcie was the matriarch and disciplinarian of her large family. By all accounts, the children were healthy and well looked after, but the boys were constantly in trouble with the law.

Michael, known as 'Mick', was the eldest of the seven boys. Born in 1953, Mick clashed with his father and was arrested for stealing a car at age 12. He went to live with his grandparents in the shadow of Long Bay Gaol, which he would later call home. Mick's grandmother doted on him, but the boy grew wild and would eventually lead his brothers into a life of crime. By the age of nine, Les Murphy had received his first conviction for car theft. Another brother, David Murphy, was convicted of armed robbery at 16.

The Murphy boys were frequently absent from school and most left as soon as they could. Like many of his brothers, Mick could not adjust to the discipline of school. He worked in a car dealership on Parramatta Road for some time before leaving his job, going on the dole and going 'thieving'. It was a pattern to be repeated from brother to brother.

'I knew them from my days at [inner Sydney suburb] Daceyville in the early 1970s,' says Ian Kennedy. 'They actually lived just down from the police station. The family were well known to police.' Police became frequent visitors to the Murphy household. 'A police car was always outside their house double parked in Binning Street [Erskineville],' remarked one detective.

In the early 1970s, Mick was a member of one of the feared skinhead 'Sharpie' gangs and was soon joined by his brothers. They terrorised pool halls and fun parlours in the city, and suburban pubs and dance venues. On weekend hundreds of street kids, including the Murphy brothers, would regularly visit a youth club set up by the Reverend Fred Nile, the director of Outreach and Evangelism for the Wesley Central Mission.

All the Murphy boys learned to box, either from local police boys clubs or from their father, who had been an amateur boxer.

'They knew how to fight,' Reverend Nile recalls. 'They went straight for the face and knew how to break a nose.' One night, Mick Murphy's mother rang Reverend Nile and asked him to pass on a message to her son. 'The police are hanging around the street, so if you're driving a stolen car, don't bring it here.'

'The Murphy kids seemed to have a continuous run of problems,' remembers Nile, who often gave character references for the Murphys at the Children's Court. The boys all had huge chips on their shoulders. They were small men, trying to act big in an often tough and uncompromising criminal world. Gary was 178 centimetres, Mick was 162 centimetres and Les was almost jockey-sized and inconsequential. Mick had the word 'love' tattooed underneath the knuckles of one hand and 'hate' on the other, a symbol perhaps of the duality of the existence on the fringes of society. Gary Murphy had 'Mum' tattooed on one forearm and 'Dad' on the other. Les had dragons on both legs, the names 'Les' and 'Dean' on his back and his daughter's name on his forearm.

Their relationships with women were sporadic, ad hoc and socially disconnected. They had many relationship between them, but there were other issues. 'We found women who had been sexually abused by these men,' says Garry Raymond. 'There was an abandoning of rules and the "I don't care about the consequences" mentality. There was no accountability in their eyes ... they were present tense thinkers. "I'll do it now and I don't care what happens tomorrow or in five years' time."

'They weren't educated and they weren't socialised. They didn't have any social mores. It was almost as if they were borders in their own families, they were "with" women but not in a relationship with them.'

By the early 1980s, Mick Murphy was in gaol, having been convicted for breaking and entering, car theft and being in the company of an armed person. Pat Murphy had a similar conviction, along with arson. Gary Murphy had numerous counts of theft against him and Les Murphy had been convicted for car theft, breaking and entering and sexual intercourse without consent in 1983. Billy Murphy was charged with stabbing and robbing a milkman.

In 1979, having been sent to Sydney's Parramatta Gaol, Mick Murphy was shocked to find a half dug escape tunnel underneath a cupboard in his 10 x 9 foot cell. When the cell's previous occupant, convicted murderer Tony Lanigan, asked for a transfer back to Parramatta from Sydney's Long Bay Gaol, he confronted Murphy and asked if he could have his old cell back.

'Why would I do that?' Murphy deadpanned. 'I like this cell – it has a big hole.'

The pair were now partners in an elaborate escape plan, and with the help of three other inmates, completed the escape tunnel through the Parramatta sandstone.

Murphy then made the mistake of phoning home and telling his family that he was getting out and would be 'home on Sunday'. His grandmother then rang the gaol to enquire 'what time' Murphy would be released. The ruse was up and the tunnel was discovered. Murphy was allegedly rewarded for revealing the existence of the tunnel with a transfer and a reduced security classification. One of the group, Stephen Stipley, was allegedly murdered in gaol in 1981 for giving up the tunnel.

But somehow, despite his extensive record, Mick Murphy was able to manipulate the system, be reclassified as a C2 prisoner and be reassigned to a low security gaol at Silverwater. On 27 December 1985, he simply walked out of the gaol. The Sydney media took great pleasure in publishing Mick Murphy's rap sheet:

Michael Patrick Murphy alias Michael Crofts, age 33, was serving a total of 24 years in gaol:

May 1972 – *aged 20, sentenced to 18 months gaol with six months non-probation for stealing a car*

August 1972 – *sentenced to 12 years for robbery in company; breaking, entering and stealing, and breaking, entering and stealing in company with an armed person*
May 1976 – *paroled*
October 1977 – *parole revoked as police seek him for various offences*
July 1978 – *returned to gaol*
September 1978 – *convicted of nine charges of breaking, entering, stealing and larceny; sentenced to eight years plus the balance of his former parole period*
November 1979 – *convicted of attempting to escape from Parramatta Gaol; sentenced to a further three years*
April 1983 – *escaped from gaol*
May 1983 – *recaptured and sent to Long Bay Gaol*
March 1984 – *sentence to one month hard labour for his escape*
January 1985 – *transferred to Cessnock medium security gaol*
November 1985 – *reclassified C2 (the second lowest security rating) and transferred to Silverwater Gaol*
December 27, 1985 – *escaped*

By that time, the Murphys had moved to a housing commission home in Delaney Drive, Doonside. The boys allegedly stole a station wagon to move the furniture and quickly became well acquainted with local police. They didn't care about getting caught because they could always intimidate witnesses not to press charges.

'The younger members of the family saw that Michael was respected in gaol and out on the streets,' says former Detective Garry Raymond, 'and that he didn't care what he did. They thought, "If I do what he does, I will be respected too and if I get sent to gaol, Michael's reputation will protect me."'

With Mick often in gaol, his brother Gary Murphy, five years his junior, would take over as disciplinarian of the family. But Gary had also been in trouble with the law for most of his life. Poor hearing and a congenital heart defect, which led to absence from school, compounded his lack of learning skills. After leaving school early, he got a steady job with a Rozelle builder where, according to his boss, he was a solid worker.

Gary's real interest was cars, however. He would work on cars for hours on end and would help friends to fix and change car parts, even if they were stolen, which often landed him in court for receiving stolen property. He owned a white EH Holden with a sunroof, mag wheels and a flashy, blue velvet interior that was 'his pride and joy.' He also kept a master set of 60 to 70 keys that fit various cars.

On the dole, Gary Murphy supplemented his income with theft, including burglary and car theft. At the time of the murder, he had a number of convictions dating back ten years for breaking, entering and theft, car theft and receiving goods in custody. He had only recently come out of Parramatta Gaol on a fines charge.

Tall, with a fair complexion, blonde hair and dimples, Gary was 'a likeable person' who got on well with the opposite sex, friends said. 'I never met anybody who was more popular with girls or has had more girlfriends than Gary,' says his lawyer Leigh Johnson. 'Remarkably, even while he's been in custody, he seems to have new girlfriends all the time.'

Quieter than Mick, but with his obvious attraction to the opposite sex, it was said that Gary 'treated women well' and that the Anita Cobby murder was 'totally out of character.'

But Gary Murphy also had a temper. After drinking or smoking marijuana with mates, he would often be involved in fights. 'His way of dealing with problems was to fight first and ask questions later,' said one friend. He had a 'hair trigger temper' and was barred for life from one of the brothers' drinking holes, the Rooty Hill RSL.

'Gary was the quiet one of the family [but he would] change like that and all of a sudden turn on you,' said another friend.

There was a duplicity to Gary Murphy's personality. In the recordings of Miss X, John Travers clearly states that Gary Murphy was part of the group that abducted, robbed and raped Anita Cobby. Witnesses place him with the group at Travers' home that burned Anita's clothes and say that he souvenired her shoes, which were never recovered.

In his statement of interview, Garry admits he was there at the crime scene, but at his trial he changed his story and said in his unsworn statement that he wasn't even there on the night of the murder – he said he spent the entire night at the Doonside Hotel. The publican later contacted police and said that he closed the hotel at 8pm on a Sunday night.

'It became clear that Gary changes his story to suit the occasion ...' remarked Garry Lynch.

One newspaper report said that during the trial, Gary Murphy even pulled a hankie out of his pocket to wipe away tears from his eyes. 'This was not true,' wrote Allan Allsopp, the Court Sherriff at the trial. 'He was not crying. In fact, he was laughing. I stood within six feet of the court dock where he sat and I saw and heard exactly what took place.'

The lives of John Travers, Mick Murdoch and the Murphy brothers finally converged in Doonside in December 1985 after Les Murphy began going out with 17-year-old Lisa Travers. A 'short, cocky' man, Les Murphy may have been one of the smallest of the family but he also had the worst temper. He'd stood in front of magistrates in Children's Court on charges of theft and car theft at the age of ten, and as a teenager Les Murphy prostituted himself at Kings Cross in pursuit of drugs and easy money.

Former Blacktown and Mt Druitt Detective Tom Sharp, who spent nine years at the Cross with the Vice Squad, remembers Les and some of his brothers standing at the famous 'wall' behind the NSW Supreme Court. 'They were up there hanging around a male brothel house called Costello's, where judges and wealthy businessmen would go to meet young male prostitutes. We'd raid it all the time and they'd be in there.'

Murphy's lawyers confirmed his client was once an 'underage male prostitute' known to be 'the frequent companion' of quite a few well known Sydney figures.

Les Murphy also left school early and spent a lot of time at pinball parlours in the city or the Cross plying his trade. Occasionally, he worked at sideshows but remained involved in criminal activities. He was a regular visitor to Yasmar Children's Court on charges of theft, riding in a stolen car and drug possession. In 1982, at the age of 19, he was convicted of two counts of having intercourse without consent and was gaoled for three years.

Released from gaol, Les tried to go straight. When the five were arrested for the Anita Cobby murder in 1986, he was the only one who was working. He and another brother had set up a maintenance business, doing repair work for a real estate agent at St Mary's. Although he had two young children with another woman, according to one friend he 'appeared to have a good thing happening' with Lisa Travers, even if she was only 17 with a child underfoot.

This was the Murphy family – railing against the world and refusing to accept their own culpability in a horrendous crime even after being found guilty and exhausting every possible appeal avenue.

GARRY RAYMOND REMEMBERS

Garry Raymond was a 21-year-old ambulance officer when he was asked by a police sergeant at a cliff rescue if he would 'go over the edge' and help the Rescue Squad secure an injured man. He did that quite a few times before the sergeant asked him if he ever thought of 'jumping ship' and joining the police.

'It sounded good to me,' Raymond says, recalling the time when he changed careers. 'I was young and keen for a new adventure … police rescue!' He even remembers what the sergeant said to him at the time: '"I'll guarantee you'll be with us in Police Rescue," he said.'

Raymond went through the police academy at Redfern, but he didn't get police rescue work straight away. He got Redfern. 'You had to do some general duties work before specialising,' he says. 'Luckily, the people at Redfern knew me because I was an "ambo" in that area,' only now things had changed.

'When I was an ambo, the indigenous population treated me royally. '"Get out of the way, Mr Raymond is coming through here," they'd shout, because I was helping them. Once I was policing them, it was "Piss off Mr Raymond, what are you doing here, you mongrel?"' he laughs.

Garry Raymond spent the next ten years in Police Rescue completing more than 1500 rescues. 'I said to my wife, "I think I know every rock at the Gap, and every car crash I know exactly what to do. I need a change to let other young blokes come in."'

Raymond decided to become a detective. He first came out to Blacktown as a general duties/rescue cop. 'I was a Senior Constable at this stage and I had the highest arrest rate of any officer in Blacktown. The reason was, I was like a kid a lolly shop and I had already done ten years in rescue, which often involved sieges. Detective Senior Sergeant Pat Toohey came downstairs and said, "Raymond, you have the highest arrest in my command!"

'"Isn't that what you're supposed to do, Serge?" I replied. "Arrest people …" He said, "I want you upstairs with the other detectives", which shows it's never too late. I did my A list as a trainee detective, and then as a general duties detective at Blacktown. The difference was, the job of a detective was slow and methodical, as opposed to getting in there and saving a life as a rescue cop. As a detective, you learned to stand back a bit and have a good look at the detail.'

Raymond and his partner Tony Waters were away in the country doing a 'lock up' at Mudgee when Anita Cobby's body was found in February 1986. 'We got a phone call to return to Sydney urgently,' Raymond recalls. 'By the time we got back, the detectives had surveyed the crime scene and recovered the body to Westmead. We were shown a series of photographs of the deceased the following day. When we got the preliminary autopsy report, we knew we were dealing with a particularly violent crime.

'It was also obvious that she had been sexually assaulted, but her fingers were broken, there was bruising and deeps cuts to her hands as if she had been trying to defend herself. Given the ferocity of the attack, the number of injuries and the bruising on both arms, it had to be more than one person involved. The striation of the bruises showed it was probably two people holding her down while others raped her.'

Tony Waters, Raymond's usual partner, was put into the detectives' team because he was the senior partner. Detective Sergeant Ian Kennedy asked Raymond and the junior detectives to 'get out there and turn the streets over and see what you can find'. Raymond was also part of a Christian street team that talked to youth at night. 'I saw a lot of things normal policing wouldn't show you,' he says, 'and I had a lot of information to pass on to the team. Some of the drug kids knew me from rehab support, so they would talk as well.'

'I went with a couple of young detectives and we visited clubs, pubs, brothels, gambling joints, hangouts for young people like the railway station. We went to the housing commission areas and did a door knock of known offenders, gang members and drug hangouts. Often, the gangs mistreated women and recruited other women to be abused as well … mainly drug gangs, some bikie gangs, but drug users clumping together for mutual benefit.

'One gang member told me, "I've been raped a dozen times, and sometimes by more than five blokes." I asked her if she had reported it and she replied, "Do you want me to get killed?"

After the details of the crime against Anita Cobby were made public, Raymond noticed a huge increase in the disquiet of the community.

'Because I knew the area, I came to know the anguish in the area … the fear, Blacktown, Seven Hills, Prospect, Toongabbie, not just the Druitt. When trains came into Blacktown Station, cars would be double parked picking up their loved ones from the station. I'd never seen that before. Women coming home from work in the city who would normally catch a bus or a taxi or walk home were now getting picked up.

'The apprehension was that whoever did this had not been arrested yet and the fear was that it might happen again. At that time, it was out that we were looking for five men so people were arming themselves with baseball bats. People would tell you straight up, "If you search my car, you'll find a butcher's knife under my seat because if those bastards turn up here, I'll carve them up."

'The public wanted to talk; no one turned us away ... they sometimes wouldn't open their door because they didn't want to be seen talking to the cops, but they would talk to us through the door. They were scared ... they mistrusted anyone they didn't know. "How do I know you are a cop?" they'd ask. They wouldn't even open the door to see our badges.

'They were hyper vigilant, almost expecting another attack. The other thing we did as police officers was to give security and safety advice to people and reassure them we were on the job.

'We had regular briefings, and typed all the intelligence up. John Travers' name came up very early,' he says. 'Most people operate within accepted social norms, not Travers. He wanted instantaneous gratification – animal, boy, girl, woman, man it didn't matter. Any rape is vicious, but this was outside the norm. Why the extra terrorisation? It was beyond the realms of what even we knew a vicious crime to be.

'We learnt a lot from Miss X's conversation with Travers that we were able to "drop" on him and the others in subsequent conversations. As an investigator, once you drop known facts on the suspects, you had them. You'd say, "I put it to you that the following happened ..." and invariably their response is "who told you that?"'

Miss X's evidence was critical. 'She got a fair backlash,' Garry says. 'Even the people in the Travers' family circle couldn't see she was doing the right thing ... it didn't surprise me. That's the way people operate ... 'don't get caught, don't cooperate with the police, don't rat on anyone.

'The other thing, they've pushed aside the normal behaviour of the community. They didn't see themselves as members of a community but separate from it. They knew exactly what they were doing ... they weren't zombies driving around in a trance. They were organised and operated as a group.

One of the most perplexing issues during the trial of the five men on trial for the abduction, rape and murder of a young woman was their behaviour in court. 'The jury was very clever in disregarding their behaviour, their laughing and sniggering … they said later that it was the behaviour of them in a group and they focused on the facts of the case. I thought the jury were extremely competent, and the judge was strong. The family was stoic and so disciplined, no yelling out or anything like that, which is amazing considering the brutality of the crime. I'm sure I would have snapped.

'It's called projected blame. "It's not me, society's to blame."

'They knew what they were doing was wrong … they hid her on the floor and covered her up at the petrol station and stopped her screaming by putting a knife in her face. If they were caught there would be consequences, but they didn't care because they had no conscience.

'The Janine Balding case, just 18 months later, shows we have a limited capacity to learn from the past,' he says. Raymond calls it the 'Adamic nature of man … that rebellious, sinful nature we inherited.'

'I was a pretty wild old boy and had a marriage break down … after that, the things I learnt in Sunday school became very real to me. In Genesis, everything was very good, God gave man a direction which they disobeyed and everything crashed around them. There was a big gulf between God and his people and that's why he sent Jesus on a rescue mission.'

Raymond became a born-again Christian and worked with the Salvation Army. After 1980, he wore two uniforms – his police uniform and a Salvation Army uniform. 'There was a riot at Long Bay Gaol and we went there and physically fought with many of the prisoners to get the gaol back under control,' he recalls. 'We were pretty exhausted at the end of it and "the Sallies" rang and asked me to go back there the next day and feed the prisoners. So I put the Salvation Army uniform on and we were giving meals to the prisoners in lockdown and they would say "thanks padre" or "thanks captain" and do a double take when they saw it was me. They would be looking at me and asking if they knew me from somewhere? Not one of them picked that the same guy who had fought them the previous day was giving them a meal.'

Garry Raymond was promoted to a command position in Manly and then Detective Inspector at Cabramatta, Wetherill Park. He worked with Operation Florida (drug detectives), terrorism risk assessment for the 2003 Rugby World Cup and from there went back to Blacktown as an Inspector. He retired there in 2004. Even when he left the force, he continued to do his part for his fellow police.

'Esther Mackay had started the Police Post Trauma Support Groups and approached me and said if I was working for the "Sallies" would I like to do some similar work with the cops? I said yes, but we remain separate from the police because a lot of traumatised cops have issues with the establishment. They often blame the policy hierarchy for their situation and so we like to keep our distance from them to remain objective. If there's disgruntlement at work and they project blame on the boss – "he didn't promote me, didn't look after me… I'm addicted to drugs, gambling, pornography … and the marriage failure and conflict with the kids" – if I'm unhappy at home, it spills over to work and vice versa. There is often a communication breakdown and we do workshops and one-on-one sessions. We have the policing faculty at UWS and we talk from experience … all those life stories and the lessons learned.'

Being a former Ambo, Raymond had experience dealing with traumatised people at the scene of an accident, as opposed to post trauma when people are dealing with critical incident stress or grief. In his new role, he would have to learn the difference.

'I learned to deal with it on the job. Going into the cops and dealing with traumatised people, you learn pretty quickly what to do and what not to do. I did a lot of reading, spoke to a lot of professionals and then observed in my colleagues what they were going through. I lectured at police rescue on pre-hospital care, including the emotional as well as physical care required.

'There is a huge gap with the preparedness for trauma … there's been a lot of research on critical incident stress (at the scene) and post-traumatic stress (after the fact), and if that is untreated PTS disorder. All the emergency services have elements of post-traumatic stress but few of us have it so bad it disorders our lives … the biggest thing in preparedness for it is to teach the young cops anatomy and physiology of their body so they know how the organs respond to trauma and its chemical bounds.

'Years ago they use to take young cadets straight into the mortuary and show them an autopsy … kids coming out of school who have never seen a body before … now, they talk them through it, explaining the role of every organ, so when they get out on the job they know what is happening to a body.

'People say we must see some terrible things, but thankfully not that often … but nobody ever tells you about the things you smell, or the things you hear, that trigger trauma. Or the silence in a child's bedroom because the child is dead in the cot, the silence where there should be sound … the things you touch, even with gloves on, pressure and temperature, where the sensory stimuli kicks in.

'Our memories are tattooed on our brains chemically. You can't say to someone to forget about it. All those memories we put into a filing cabinet – some at the front and some at the back – and we leave them there. Some people can go to that cabinet and get out the file and remember all the details, others know the files are there but they don't want to look at it. It's a protective measure because remembering the details of certain crimes arouses the chemicals in the body – the fight and flight chemistry – that makes people respond the way they do.'

Raymond used to drop in and visit with Garry and Grace Lynch in the years after the trial. 'If I was in the area, I would ring ahead and drop in for a cuppa and talk to them,' he says. 'Let them talk it through, which was important. Garry was a very spiritual person … he was very aware of the presence of God even in the worst circumstances. Grace was a little quieter and didn't say too much, but she was a woman of enormous faith.

'I once asked Garry how he coped with everything. Was there something in his background that had prepared him for this? "No," he said. "Nothing could prepare you for something like this."'

CHAPTER FOURTEEN

The Detectives

The only pressure we put on ourselves was that we did the job right. We knew it was our job and we knew we were going to do our best to solve it. As far as I was concerned, it was only a matter of time ... these were not master criminals who had covered their tracks ... and with what we had from the initial crime scene, the witnesses to the abduction and the information coming in, it was only a matter of time.

Former detective, Graham Rosetta

The murder of Anita Cobby was totally out of the experience of the community and the investigating team in terms of what happened to one victim. It changed many lives, including the men and women trusted to investigate it.

In 1986, Debbie Wallace was a 26-year-old uniformed policewoman at Blacktown Station. She admits she was 'in awe' of the close-knit group of detectives who worked in the upstairs office, perhaps knowing subconsciously she too would end up there one day. That feeling was confirmed when Homicide detectives joined the local team to investigate the murder of Anita Cobby. As a team, they were literally awe-inspiring for the young policewoman.

'I remember the detectives' office looked like a scene out of the TV show Barney Miller,' Wallace later wrote. 'You could smoke in the building in those days and one of the first things that I noticed was the way the detectives always seemed to have a cigarette dangling from the corner of the mouth, typing away on a manual typewriter, the top button of their shirts undone and the tie knot pulled down.'

'We did the entire case on manual typewriters,' recalls Garry Heskett. 'There were no computers at that stage, no CSI and no DNA, just good hard slogging yakka. Most of the detectives involved in the investigation were from working class backgrounds, unlike today where it is a real middle class profession. Kevin Raue may have had a tertiary qualification;

he went off and did a Justice and Administration course at Charles Sturt University – we call it the 'bricklayers' course' for detectives. I was the most junior detective on the case, but I had eight years' experience compared to today when you can be a detective sergeant after six years and an inspector after ten.'

The nature of policing has changed enormously in the years since the 1986 case, but some things never change. 'Homicide investigations, like most criminal investigation work, is very contradictory and very fragmented,' Heskett says. 'It's about good people doing bad things and bad people doing good things. The victim is not always a decent person; neither are the perpetrators always bad people.

'The murder of Anita Cobby, however, was a classical needless crime where the victim was a decent, good person from a very stable family and the perpetrators were all underprivileged petty criminals from disadvantaged families ...'

It was unfathomable, Heskett says. Why would they do this? Why did this happen to this poor girl? 'The fact that five young men savaged her and had their way with her for several hours before cutting her throat, she had never done wrong by society and was a good, decent human being.' He still shakes his head about it.

'We wanted to make a difference, but our feet were squarely on the ground. None of us advocated to the neo liberal rubbish that you could be whatever you wanted to be and achieve whatever you wanted to achieve if you just tried hard enough.' That dimension of policing has changed enormously, he says. 'Now it's more about quantity than quality. I don't know if an incident like this happened today it would receive the same attention from the police, not that police today don't care, because they do, but I wonder how the average police officer could work eight weeks straight.'

One of the most important changes to policing came from what detectives learned about dealing with grief, and dealing with traumatised families, in the Cobby case. 'Police always responded to the needs and rights of victims,' says Heskett. 'However, due to continued procedural changes – concentrating on procedures and processes – police were often focused on the outcome of their results.'

The Cobby investigation, and the contact with the Lynch family, would change all their perceptions on how victims of crimes, especially homicide, should be treated.

'I'd be lying to you if I said it wasn't the toughest case I worked on because it was,' says Graham Rosetta. 'Everyone would say that. As terrible as the case was, I never allowed myself to dwell on things.'

Graham 'Rosie' Rosetta is not one to dwell too much on the past. As Debbie Wallace later noted '[Rosetta] didn't say much but when he spoke you listened and you learned … [he was] the first in and the last to leave'. Rosetta maintains the only pressure the team of detectives put on themselves was to solve the case.

'There was no pressure on us from the media or the government. I can't subscribe to that, because you can't allow yourself to be under pressure because you cut corners and you get desperate and it's possible that you overlook things. I knew Neville Wran at the time came out and commented about the case – as NSW Premier that was his right, advocating the death penalty and such – but we had no pressure from our operational superiors to go out and solve the case.'

Does Rosetta think the murderers will ever get out? 'In terms of gravity of the crime and acts of bastardy, there was a parallel with the Janine Balding case in 1988 and yet, there are still people pushing to have those offenders released from gaol. John Travers is only 49 years old and could still do a lot of damage. He has a lot of years in front of him and they should be spent in gaol.'

You never know how people in five or ten years' time will think, Rosetta says. 'If anyone ever thought about having any pity for them, in terms of release at some stage for them, then they just have to remember what Justice Maxwell said at their sentencing.

'I just hope we have governments strong enough to act if they do try and get out. The case will still be strong enough in the memory to take to the street if they did try and release them.'

'The case was the most dreadful for everyone involved,' says Tony Waters. 'Stop and think about the victim … Anita Cobby, Miss Western Suburbs, a nurse working for the community, and then the horrendous nature of her death and how she was found.'

It was a tough investigation to work on, he says, but the detectives formed a great bond, having worked together for years. 'As well as getting a good reaction to the appeals for assistance, you also get the negative reaction with people wanting to vent. There was some ridiculous things reported and you knew you had to go out there and follow every blind alley lead.'

The hard work they had to do also produced their lighter moments ... call it police 'black humour'. Remembers Waters, 'Early in the investigation, we were out one night searching for the suspects in a squad car and we hadn't done any good. The media were out the front of the police station in droves, searching for a story. One of the detectives in the back seat put a coat over his head and the media went into overdrive. It created absolute havoc until he removed the coat from his head and the media realised who it was. It was just one way to release the tension ... the media coverage was phenomenal. We hadn't seen anything like it.'

It was a light moment in a grim case. 'The terrible part was having to watch the Lynch family go through the whole thing again at Glebe Coroner's Court, then at Darlinghurst and of course again when Les Murphy was granted a retrial. Having led a number of murder investigations during my time, it is part of the job you never get used to [the impact on the family]. The Lynch family were amazing people ... they were the real heroes.'

The Cobby case saw the very worst and best of human nature at work, says Garry Raymond, who now works as a police chaplain. 'The mob mentality and the community coming together seeking justice ... the duality of it all ... can't lose sight of the fact that a beautiful girl lost her life. There is no justice in that, other than that the people responsible are in gaol.

'There is a tendency to turn Anita into an angel, a saint, but she was an ordinary person going about her ordinary duties and that makes what happened to her extraordinary enough. There is no need to put her on a pedestal, but people still remember her that way. I think a big part of that was because she was a nurse. She was healing the sick, and those hands that tried to stop her own rape and the knife cutting her throat had bandaged people and resuscitated people and helped doctors knit people back together again.'

The media always said 'nurse Anita Cobby' as if it was part of her name. 'That was the tragedy of the case,' Raymond says. 'Someone doing so much good in the community, no longer here to do what they love.'

But it's a story that continues to blossom and grow. 'On one case I was involved in, we were searching for a lost child in the bush and we were doing an "emu search" with choppers overhead, and I came across a cow paddy. Growing out of that was the most beautiful bush orchard you would want to see. I remember talking to Garry Lynch about it, and I said that was like you … out of the terrible murder of your daughter has grown this beautiful flower. It was as if it was a seed, covered in all this muck and bacteria, feeding off all this and cracking open to grow this beautiful flower.

'There are a lot of things in life we don't want to talk about because they are so hard … sexual assault, suicide, murder … but when we did bring them up and talk about them, some amazing things happen. We can learn from the past … '

'I wouldn't want to say it was the worst murder ever and put it in a category all of its own,' says Ian Kennedy who led the task force. 'Any murder is terrible, no matter who the person is.

'Alan Coote, the publican of the Gladstone Hotel at Dulwich Hill in Sydney, was a former detective in north western NSW in the early 1970s at the time of the murder of Virginia Morse. I met him at a function and he was very upset with me. "Did you say that the Cobby case was the worst murder ever?" he asked. I never said that, I told him. I said the Cobby case was "one of the worst murders in NSW and ranks up there with the murder of Virginia Morse in 1973 and others."

I knew Alan – he is the cousin of rugby league legend Ron Coote, who was my next door neighbour at Maroubra – and I knew he had worked on the Morse case and captured the murderers, Allan Baker and Kevin Crump. He took offence to that assertion, but he was fine when I explained what I said.'

Its shows how long these men and women trusted with investigating crimes as heinous as this carry the memories with them. Every crime is important to them because there are victims to consider.

The Janine Balding murder, for example, happened just 18 months after Anita Cobby's, Kennedy adds. 'Kevin Raue worked on that one too and I remember saying to him, "What the hell is going on out west?" Here we were, with locals wanting to hang the Cobby murderers in front of the court house, and then we have another group of people committing this murder. Surely they knew the cops were going to capture them, given what happened with the Cobby case …

'Criminals don't think that way,' he adds. 'They hadn't learned anything and I don't think they have learned anything still. Today, crime is more prevalent … [there are] ethnic gangs made up of disaffected people who haven't adapted to the Australian way of life. Heroin is on the decrease but ice use is rampant. Guns are banned, but too many people are getting killed with knives – young kids, and even girls, are carrying knives – and we seem to be lax in sentencing knife crimes. Gaols are full and criminals are getting out on bail too easily …

'I don't even think about the killers,' Kennedy says. 'Years ago I use to wonder about them but I've moved on and that's in the past. I don't need to reminisce.'

Most of the detectives who worked on the Anita Cobby case are now retired from the force. Graham Rosetta was the first to retire in 1989, following a work related injury, and now lives in southern NSW. Ian Kennedy still works in the justice system, but he retired as a detective in 1999 and pursued a coaching career in representative rugby union. The negative affect of policing finally wore Garry Heskett down – he relocated to the NSW mid north coast in 2004 where he works as a sports injury therapist. Kevin Raue became a publican, as Paul Rynne did for a time, while also setting up crime task forces in the South Pacific. Paul Davies married Lyn Bradshaw, Anita's nursing colleague, although the marriage later faltered. Chris O'Toole lives in the country. Garry Raymond continues his association with his colleagues as a police chaplain, talking to police about work related and personal issues. After a couple of tough years, Tony Waters continues to fight the good fight back to premium health.

In her own words, Debbie Wallace was only 'on the periphery of the investigation', fielding calls coming in from the public when she was asked to re-enact Anita Cobby's final hours on the train.

Wallace says she felt a connection with Anita; she was roughly the same age, also recently separated from her husband, and there was a slight physical resemblance as well, although when she followed in Anita's footsteps, it was dark and the road poorly lit. On the night of the re-enactment, cameras were not allowed to follow her after leaving the railway station. Detectives followed in a car not too far behind. That's when the enormity of what happened to Anita Cobby hit home.

'Anita would never walk home again, never see her family or friends, never go back to work.' Wallace had walked home from work many times from Westmead Station. 'This could have been any girl …' she later wrote.

Debbie Wallace was not just any girl, especially in a male-dominated profession such as the NSW Police. After the re-enactment, the Cobby task force invited her to join the investigative team. She learned quickly.

One important lesson Wallace took from the Cobby case when she became a detective in 1989 was the way the 'hardened detectives' on the case connected emotionally with the Cobby family, and to Anita herself. Rather than remaining aloof and distant in order to remain professional and impartial during the investigation, which was often perceived to be part of police culture, 'I realise now that by taking time to know the family and to understand the crime's impact, it made the detectives more focused and more determined to find the answer to the questions … "why?" and "how?"'

Wallace felt 'too awkward' to approach and talk to the Lynch family during the case because she was close enough to see how the murder of Anita had affected all of them. She later worked on the Anita and Beyond exhibition in the early 2000s and got to know the family well. 'Perhaps in some strange way, their greatest contribution to our community may just give us the example of strength needed should we/others ever face such a significant loss in our own lives.'

Debbie Wallace also spares a thought for the families of the men who murdered Anita, who were 'hounded and abused' through no fault of their own. 'There were people who deserved to be punished, but there are a lot of innocent people who get hurt in these things too.'

By the end of the 1990s, Wallace became Chief Inspector and Crime Manager at Cabramatta before being transferred to the Asian Organised Crime Squad in 2003. In 2006, she was made Superintendent, and in later the years later, headed the Middle Eastern Organised Crime Squad.

Not bad for a Western Sydney girl, much like Anita Cobby.

CHAPTER FIFTEEN

THE WITNESS

'The witnesses in Newton Road provided a huge early breakthrough. The eye witness account of the kidnap by men in a car … it was not the most accurate description, but remember they were scared kids. It showed the community spirt … they wanted to help … they gave us the first clues.
Former detective, Ian Kennedy

On the night of 2 February 1986, the McGaughey family were in their Newton Road home in suburban Blacktown. 16-year-old Linda and older brother John, 22, were watching TV in the family home. Another sibling, Paul, a talented local footballer then aged 20, was out with his girlfriend at Blacktown Drive-In, not far from Reen Road where certain events that summer night would impact all their lives.

It was young Linda who heard the scream from the front room of the house, closest to the street, just before 10pm. The unmistakeable sound of a young woman's scream pierced the still night. Linda ran to the driveway just in time to see a young woman struggling with a group of men and being dragged into a car. Linda called out to her brother John that a girl was 'in trouble' out the front, and the pair ran onto the front lawn of their home. As the young woman disappeared inside the car John, barefoot and in shorts, took off on foot after them.

He got as close as the back door handle of the car before it sped off into the night. He was close enough to see the male passengers in the back of the car turn around and laugh at him.

'I arrived home shortly after,' remembers Paul McGaughey, now a 50-year-old father of three who still lives in the western suburbs where he grew up all those years ago. There was a commotion in the street when he arrived – neighbours had come out on to the street after they too had heard the screams and yelling and car revving – and he was surprised to see his entire family standing out in the middle of the street.

'Linda and John told me that a girl had been grabbed off the street.

When I asked what sort of car it was, they said it was a HT or HG Holden. Being a car enthusiast, I knew the difference between the two but the general consensus that night was the men were in a 'dirty white' HG Holden. I immediately drove off with my girlfriend still in the front seat, not really knowing in which direction they may have gone, but somehow I ended up at the top of Reen Road. I had just been to the drive-in and I knew it was a 'lover's lane' type hangout, and so I drove down to the bottom of the street.'

There were a number of cars at the bottom of that poorly lit road that night but Paul can still remember them … 'a red Sigma and an old Falcon,' he recalls and then, some distance off, what appeared to be a grey Holden. 'I drove past the Holden, but it wasn't a HG model and so I wasn't sure,' Paul says. 'I did a U-turn and used a handheld spotlight I had from one of our fishing trips to light up the car and scan the paddock behind it. There appeared to be no one in the car.' Only later, during the trial, did he learn that the five men were hiding in the long grass with their victim until the light moved away.

30 years on from that hot February night, Paul McGaughey still contemplates what might have been. 'I was 20 and fit and had no fear,' he says. 'I was so close …' Perhaps today, with mobile phones and CCTV cameras, the situation might have been different, he says. He also knows he could have kicked a hornet's nest with his girlfriend and he would probably have been no match for five young men on a blood lust. But still, a day doesn't go by when he doesn't think about that night … and Anita Cobby.

That Sunday night, Paul arrived back home about 90 minutes after going on his search and two police officers were talking to his mother, brother and sister. His mother had called the authorities while Paul was out on the road looking around Blacktown. 'There was very little to go on,' he admits. The vague description of a car, some screams in the street – perhaps it was a domestic issue gone wrong or a prank? Those scenarios changed when a woman's body was found in Reen Road the following Tuesday.

'I was devastated,' Paul says. 'We all were. I knew straight away it was the young woman Linda and John had seen taken off the street, the person I had been looking for on the Sunday night.' On Tuesday afternoon, when news of the discovery hit the media, Paul contacted the police, who were already in the process of identifying the body.

'That night two detectives came to our house,' Paul remembers. 'Detectives Ian Kennedy and Paul Rynne. They wanted to know where I had seen the car on Reen Road.'

And so started a series of events that would transform the lives of the McGaughey family, the wider Western Sydney community and ultimately the nation. Linda and John still have difficulty talking about the case, but the events of 1986 and the turbulent years when afterwards when the men were brought to trial, have washed over Paul and in many ways, transformed him.

'The media coverage of the Anita Cobby case doesn't let you forget,' he says 'and in many ways, they shouldn't let us forget. It's important that everyone knows the consequences of that crime. A young woman was raped and murdered. Five men were gaoled for the rest of their natural lives. Life in gaol means life.'

John and Linda were asked by the task force to visit a Sydney hypnotherapist in an effort to glean a clearer description of the men in the car. 'The detectives were fantastic,' Paul says. 'They really treated Linda with kid gloves because she was so young …' Private security guards were hired to watch the McGaughey household while the men responsible were being rounded up. 'We didn't know who was involved in the crime and what the backlash would be from family members or supporters of the men.' The family was on tenterhooks until the end of the trial a year later, right up to the moment when the words 'never to be released' were uttered by Justice Alan Maxwell at the NSW Supreme Court.

The McGaughey siblings were each asked to give evidence at the trial, an experience Paul remembers as being difficult for everyone involved. His employers at the time, Cumberland Newspaper Group, were very understanding and gave him the time off he needed. In the witness room before taking the stand, the McGaugheys sat with Grace and Garry Lynch, who each took turns to sit with the siblings, sometimes holding their hands for comfort.

'The Lynches were incredibly nice people,' Pauls remembers. 'Very kind and understanding. In the years after the trial, we would run into them all the time – we continued to live in Blacktown and even shared the same doctor at one stage. They were always very nice to us; generous, caring people … '

Compare this quiet respite to the scene inside and outside the courtroom … the mobs calling for the hanging of the men responsible for the crime, the snickering of the five young men in the courtroom as the evidence of what happened that night was tabled. The fact that some of the people responsible for the crime were the same age as Paul – barely 21 years old – was not lost on him. 'They were guys my age,' Paul says incredulously, 'with that pack mentality. What was it? Their upbringing? Where they lived? I grew up in that area so it wasn't just that. You couldn't blame the media or the Internet and video games because they weren't even invented. It was unbelievable … '

There was an interesting dynamic happening out on the Blacktown streets at that time, he says. The people protesting on the street when Travers, Murdoch and Murphy were first brought to Blacktown – with their misspelt signs, stubbies and thongs – were from the same suburbs as the killers. 'They were not only protesting against what the men had done, they were also protesting on behalf of the community. It was almost "how dare you do this to Doonside and Blacktown? You come from this community too …"'

Thankfully, if anything, the protests showed that the men responsible for the crime didn't represent the wider community. Paul still shakes his head at the people who protected the five men from being captured by the police. What were they thinking? How did they live with themselves?

Paul was not in court the day the verdict was handed down. 'I had promised a mate that I would help him out on a truck run. I was listening to John Laws on the radio when he read out the verdict … guilty. I immediately felt a sense of relief. It was all over.'

Working in marketing and advertising sales also opened Paul's eyes to the commercial realities of the media. 'Unfortunately, a lot of stories were generated to sell advertising,' he says matter-of-factly. It was the way of the world, he learned, the power of the corporate dollar.

The impact of the Cobby case was also a 'wakeup call' for the young man that the world was not necessarily a nice place, a shattering realisation for such a young group of people. 'Horrific cases like this only happen in America, I thought, not in Blacktown. What happened made everyone aware of the evil that lurks under the surface of suburban life, and made us all a little more cautious and wary.'

Although Paul says the crime didn't come to define their lives, the death of Anita Cobby did shape his future. After selling advertising for Cumberland Newspapers and working with local media identity Con Constantine on the establishment of Parklea Markets, and the running of Constantine's local *Guardian* newspaper. Paul moved on to producing television ads for CH7 and advertising sales for *The Sun Herald*. He also became involved in marketing for the Pepsi Company and its subsidiary Smiths Chips. In the early '90's, his work in the media had introduced him to another media identity, Graham McNeice, who produces films for his own production company (GMP, Graham McNeice Productions) and for Foxtel.

'I worked with Graham on his Crime Investigation: Australia series,' Paul says – the irony of being a Crown witness in the Anita Cobby case and then working on the 2006 episode was not lost on him. 'I assisted Graham when needed … the house used for the episode on the Sef Gonzales family murders was actually my house. The floor plan was pretty much the same as the murder scene.' Paul even took a small role in the episode as a helpful neighbour, but for the most part was happy to stay behind the scenes.

Paul was always interested in the justice aspect of policing, especially after the trial and getting to know the arresting detectives Ian Kennedy, Graham Rosetta, Keith Raue, Keith Rynne and Garry Heskett. 'We shared many beers together at Blacktown Sportsman's Hotel,' Paul recalls, 'and I was absolutely amazed at the job they did. I was successful in my own work, but I wasn't fulfilled or happy in it, so at age 35 I bit the bullet and changed careers.'

In 2002, Paul joined the NSW Justice system as a compliance officer. He now deals directly with the integration and supervision of offenders back into the community, acting as 'the eyes and the ears' of the court to make sure ex-prisoners are compliant with the respective conditions of their release. He has undergone extensive training and education for such a role and believes that successful re-introduction into the community depends on an honest and open rapport between both parties. With community and family support, rehabilitation is the main goal, but Paul is also a realist.

'There is recidivism among prisoners,' he admits, easily identifying those people who use the justice system like a revolving door. He is a strong advocate of truth in sentencing. 'If you commit the crime, you do the time,' he says. 'It's written in black and white.'

The key is early intervention, he says, especially with offenders in the juvenile justice system. Identifying offenders at a young age, accessing the proper counselling (such as anger management) and utilising the correct referral systems (especially with drug counselling) are integral parts of that success.

Paul rarely thinks about the five men responsible for the Anita Cobby murder. When he heard that Michael Murdoch had found God he commented, 'If you ever want to find God, gaol is a good place to find Him. It's a shame he didn't find God before he committed the crime.'

'The only way they will get out of gaol is if we forget what happened,' he admits. 'When the story becomes "fish and chip wrappings" then they will have a chance to get out and then God help us if they do.'

'Those young wimps who went into gaol 30 years ago are now entering their 50s. They will be wimpy old men – perhaps in wheelchairs – but they will still have that underlying pack mentality and present a threat to society. They will also be heavily institutionalised by then, so best leave them in gaol where they belong.'

Paul thinks of Anita often. His daughter is undertaking legal studies and knows the case backwards. 'Anita Cobby was "the girl next door",' Paul McGaughey says. 'I never met her, but by the end of the trial, I felt I had known her all my life. May she forever rest in peace.'

CHAPTER SIXTEEN

The Media

'There's a saying: "I know how you feel" or "I know how so-and-so must have felt". But it's nonsense. Really we don't. Unless you are actually in the subject's shoes then one can only hazard a guess as to how they feel. When the farmer found the body in the cow paddock at Prospect and the photos of the scene came back to the office, a few coppers standing in the middle of what seemed like nowhere, such a desolate God forsaken place … trees, fence posts strung with barbed wire, empty roads, long grass … you were suddenly overwhelmed by a feeling of absolute pity for the poor young girl, trying to imagine the hell she must have gone through.'

John Benaud, former editor of *The Sun* newspaper

The media played an active role in the Anita Cobby case, from the first horrific reports of her body being found in the paddock at Reen Road, the appeal from police, family and friends for information leading to the capture of the men responsible and the coverage of the trial and subsequent appeals in various media formats. As a result, for thousands of people in Western Sydney, the state of NSW and indeed the entire country, the life and death of Anita Cobby has remained very much in the public consciousness.

Unlike most other murders that are reported and then largely forgotten, the public identified emotionally with Anita and sympathised with her family. The reaction to the Cobby case by the media, the police, the law community and the greater public, however, was extraordinary. Nationwide public interest in this case was unprecedented … during the trial, newspaper and television news ratings increased dramatically.

Sometimes the media got it wrong, but more often than not, the various mediums correctly communicated the multifaceted impact the crime had on everyone … the stark tragedy of a young life so needlessly taken, the pain her family and friends suffered, the earnestness of the police investigation and, finally, both the angst and jubilation the community felt when the five offenders were captured and brought to justice. Family friend

Anne King observed, 'People got involved in [the case] because of the type of nature Anita had. I think it was also the way the media portrayed Anita. They got her personality correctly.'

'From the date of the murder until the arrest of the last two offenders was three weeks and five days,' remembers Ian Kennedy. 'During this time, the media coverage of the murder never wavered. It was also because she was a nurse – a profession that helps all people; a lovely, attractive girl so cruelly treated and her injuries were absolutely ghastly.'

From the first day, Garry and Grace Lynch felt the full brunt of media intrusion into their lives, but they learned to embrace the media – making themselves available for interviews and appealing directly to the camera – in an effort help police solve the case. It was not an easy thing for anyone to do, let alone parents grieving for their murdered daughter.

In his autobiography, Garry wrote:

'On Tuesday night we watched the news on television and to our horror we saw a helicopter shot of the boiler paddock with police vehicles and ambulances everywhere. The cameras zoomed in and panned over a roof of a van to reveal Anita's beautiful naked body lying face down in the grass. The commentary said her head had nearly been severed from ear to ear as if by a garden spade. The shot was shown a few times on television before we protested and then it was withdrawn.'

At 6am the following morning, the Lynches had a camera crew on their doorstep. Garry politely asked them to return at a more respectable hour, 8.30am. The Lynch family were the personification of patience and good manners. Grace and Garry Lynch faced the media with dignity and strength and gave their daughter humanity … nobility even.

'It was very hard because we never had anything to do with the media or police before,' Grace said, 'but we knew we had to.' Garry was later to write, '…the police, the media and the general public were to treat us with great kindness.'

As head of the task force, Detective Sergeant Ian Kennedy was charged with the responsibility of constantly briefing the media. 'I remember telling Garry Lynch we didn't have any leads,' he says. '"We need you to talk to the press," I told him. "All we can do is control when they talk to you … if someone rings you at an uncomfortable hour, you give me their name and I will speak to their bosses and they will be kicked off the inquiry.

'"I don't want you to refuse to talk to anyone if they are polite …" I asked, and Garry did it to a tee. That's why people came forward because of the constant publicity. In some murders, the amount of press given to a crime can be a hindrance. In our case, it became the catalyst for information coming in that helped solve the case.

'In the end, the murder may never have been solved if Miss X had not come forward and she did so, not because of the reward on offer but because of the media coverage which outlined [Anita's] injuries and disgusted another female. So while the media were at times intrusive, persistent and even a nuisance, they ultimately were responsible for its successful conclusion … and of course because of the very hard working group of police involved.'

On the Friday before the funeral, John Laws had revealed details from the autopsy report on Radio 2GB. In his haste to broadcast, the report allegedly stated that the victim's sexual organs had been 'butchered' and her shoulders dislocated, which was untrue. When it was suggested that the report was based on his post mortem, Dr Joe Malouf said, 'It certainly didn't come from me.' It was later determined that the report came via a leak in the police media unit.

The Lynches didn't hear the broadcast but many of their friends and neighbours did. Garry Lynch later wrote that the family was 'terribly upset about the description of knife and barbed wire cuts to her body, particularly how there had been penetration and lacerations to her anus.'

'Initially I hated John Laws for making those details public,' Garry admitted, ' … but later I thought that at least it meant people in our country learnt of the horror of what can happen when a man, or a group of men, go berserk.'

There was more pain ahead for the Lynch family. On Sunday 9 February, a week after Anita was walking home from Blacktown Station, the police staged a re-enactment of Anita's final hours on the train and walking home. It was one of the first times police used a media strategy to reach out to the public about an unsolved crime such as this, and it led to vital information about the attack being passed on to them.

To increase the authenticity of the re-enactment for the young policewoman playing Anita, the murdered woman's nursing friends were asked to select similar clothes to those worn by Anita on the night she was murdered. Grace and Garry Lynch were particularly unhappy.

'On seeing the footage we were very upset,' said Garry, 'because they never consulted us and they had dressed the police woman in the clothes that Anita would never have worn, and the camera seemed to concentrate on the sway of the woman's hips … we could have lent them some of Anita's clothes, but it was a minor incident, I suppose, but we felt it insulted Anita and implied things that simply were not so.'

The Cobby case hit at the very heart of public fear … abduction, rape and murder. Garry Lynch himself described the murder of his daughter as 'one of the worst crimes against womanhood'. The re-enactment had touched a raw nerve; the angle of the video camera following the young policewoman focused on the bottom half of her body and had inadvertently sexualised the scenes. It was indicative of the very delicate line the media and the investigation team had to walk.

'We got to know the press very well,' says Ian Kennedy. 'Simon Bouda and Julia Shepherd at *The Sun*, Max Uechtritz at the ABC and Jennifer Cooke at the *Sydney Morning Herald* … it was good to get to know the type of people they were, whether they could be trusted, whether they were honest. Julia was accepted by the family; she asked us if it was OK if she went and spoke to people. She didn't just rock up unannounced and hassle people.'

'The press, after a while, realised the Lynches were great people and didn't ask them stupid questions or try and interview them at unreasonable hours. A lot of the press dropped off after a few weeks because nothing was happening … and those that hung around knew how to interview them. They asked us if they could question Garry and Grace and I said, "Do it politely", and they understood.'

The Sun newspaper was one of two Sydney afternoon newspapers in circulation in the 1980s. Often regarded as the poor relation to the Murdoch-run Daily Mirror, the Fairfax owned tabloid would go out of business just two years later, the victim of an increasingly ruthless media market. The coverage of the Cobby case, in many regards, provided *The Sun* with a last hurrah in ground breaking journalism, which was in no small way because of its erstwhile editor, former Test cricketer John Benaud, the younger brother of Richie Benaud.

'*The Sun* was an afternoon tabloid and therefore easily abused as sensational by the broadsheeters,' John Benaud says. 'But every news outlet has a little sensationalism in the blood. It is true Anita's killing could have been sensationalised, but why would you? Once you knew the horrific brutality of the crime, pretty much the moment the body was found, and observed the dignity of her parents, the very gentle Grace and Garry Lynch, then just the straight facts would do. To sensationalise would, I think, have brought a roar of disapproval from the public.'

Anita had been an entrant in the Miss Australia Quest, which was organised by the NSW Spastic Centre and, coincidentally, promoted by *The Sun* newspaper. 'I suppose that got us a little more "involved" too,' says Benaud. 'Anita was also a nurse. So, a beautiful young lady, in life's full bloom, helped the handicapped kids and healed the sick … an angel in the eyes of the public. There was a lot of emotion ... '

Under Benaud's editorship, *The Sun* developed 'a steely resolve' to do all in everything in their power to assist in bringing the killers to justice. 'This was not just another crime,' he says. '…You could sense a surge of urgency to "get the bastards".

'The police roundsman, Simon Bouda, now with Channel Nine, was our main reporter,' remembers Benaud, 'an absolute professional, and well connected to the police force. But we decided on a team approach and linked to him a female journalist named Julia Sheppard. She came to know Anita's parents very well. Between them, they'd offer briefings at the start and end of every day that kept us on top of the story.'

The day after the five men were convicted, *The Sun* produced a special edition in which the first nine pages of the newspaper were devoted to aspects of the crime and its impact on Sydney, especially the western suburbs. Circulation increased by ten per cent. Benaud admits some may have regarded this approach as 'cashing in' on the story but he says the public had 'a loving respect' for Anita Cobby and that there was 'a chemistry' between her and the public that heightened their awareness and outrage. It was important that the paper not only cover the story but do it justice and give it the prominence it deserved.

That 'chemistry' between Anita Cobby and the public may be best summed up by the actions of local man Jackson Mashinini who stopped in at the Darlinghurst Court on 16 June 1987 when the guilty verdicts were brought in by the jury foreman. The Sydney bus driver, who had never met Anita Cobby or the Lynch family, was photographed skipping with delight outside the court when the verdict was handed down with a look of absolute joy on his face. That image was splashed all cover the morning newspapers and won an award for press photography at year's end.

'That image was like the "dancing man" filmed in a Sydney street on the day World War II ended,' says Ian Kennedy. The Anita Cobby case was a bit like that too … the elderly bus driver celebrating the end of something horrible and terrible with happiness and joy.

Contrasting themes were often played out under the media glare, but the Anita Cobby investigation could never be oversimplified as being a simple case of 'good versus evil.' The Cobby case has always had an incredible local significance for family, friends and the communities of Western Sydney. Anita came from Western Sydney, but then so did the killers.

In demonising the men responsible for her murder, many people in Western Sydney were labelled and looked down upon during that time, especially those living on the margins of society. The problem with objectifying the men as monsters is that it reduces their responsibility as rational thinking human beings. They were, in fact, five young men who made up their minds to go down a particular path – they knew the difference between right and wrong and still acted on their bloodlust.

At the other end of the spectrum, the media tried to turn Anita into an angel. She was a nurse, someone who cared for others; a daughter, a sister, a wife and a friend – and, in the words of Garry Heskett, her name has now become 'a byword for the absolute extremes of human nature'. The great irony, of course, is that these two worlds – of monsters and angels – lived side by side in neighbouring suburbs. When Garry Lynch was called 'a saint' by a member of the community, he wryly observed, 'What a bloody horrible way to have to qualify to be one.'

In 2002, the Anita and Beyond art project was created specifically for the communities of Western Sydney to perhaps try to come to terms with many of these conflicting issues that still resonated out of the events of February 1986. The art project was guided by a Western Sydney curatorium, featured Western Sydney artists for a Western Sydney audience. The goal was to provide the opportunity and mechanism for the community to understand complex issues, views and perspectives … 'informing people how a murder and its aftermath affect the whole family and friends.'

Originally the exhibition was conducted by the Casual Powerhouse

Arts Centre and Liverpool Museum before Penrith Regional Gallery and the Lewers Bequest came on board as the co-producing and presentation partner. According to director John Kirkman, the exhibition was an 'ambitious synergy of social history and contemporary visual arts practices [that] aims to celebrate a life lost and a legacy both potent and affirming.' It featured works of art, video presentations and even displays of items relating directly to Anita – her artwork, her school notebooks, her Miss Western Sydney sash.

In the 30 years since the events of that hot February Sunday, the investigation has been the subject of books, several documentaries, an art exhibition and even a stage play and film. Many authors have covered the Cobby case in anthologies of Australian crime. Julia Sheppard's book, Someone Else's Daughter, published in 1991 sold more than 150,000 copies. Producer Graham McNeice featured the Anita Cobby murder in the first season of his Crime Investigation: Australia series in 2005, interviewing Garry and Grace Lynch and most of the detectives on the case. The crime also attracted international documentarians, with British and Canadian production companies also featuring the murder on a global scale. Gordon Graham's chilling 1990s play The Boys was partially based on the powerful relationships between the five men who took part in the Cobby murder and was turned into a 1998 film starring David Wenham and Toni Collette. The list goes on.

As psychologist Russell Hogg later noted, however, the most important part the media played in the Cobby case was not just in covering the investigation, but to 'humanise' Anita Cobby as a victim, thereby giving her life 'meaning and resonance for many who did not know her.'

CHAPTER SEVENTEEN

The Killers

'The harm done to Travers when he was a child almost certainly, bit by bit, led to his present situation … it does seem to me Mr Travers was beaten into a situation where insecure aggression was his only coping mechanism against a (perceived) hostile world … I suppose if one takes into account the terribly disturbed personality and then considered the effect of intoxication with these substances upon him, one gets a picture of grossly abnormal mental functioning, in the general sense of perception of right and wrong, and the ability to control himself.'
Psychologist, Hugh Jolly

After their arrest, the five men accused of killing Anita Cobby were remanded to nearby Parklea Gaol, north of Blacktown. Following John Travers' decision to plead guilty to the crime, which effectively threw the other four men under a legal bus, there was a falling out amongst the killers. In March 1988, Travers was spirited away to a maximum security wing at Maitland Correctional Centre, near Newcastle on the NSW north coast, before being shifted to Goulburn in southwest NSW.

Following their conviction for abduction, assault, robbery, rape and murder, Gary and Mick Murphy were placed in special protection in Long Bay. Michael Murdoch and Les Murphy would soon join them there, segregated from the rest of the population.

By the end of the 1980s, having exhausted their respective appeals, all five were in maximum security wings in various NSW gaols. Although they would each spend the best part of a decade segregated from the rest of the gaol population – not because they were a danger to society but because they were in danger from other prisoners – they were not employed to do any specific duties, and they passed their time 'watching television, playing table tennis or snooker.'

The five were called many things during the media blitz of the initial investigation and the trial … accused, offenders, animals, rapists and finally killers. Although they were eager to give their version of events to investigating detectives, minimising their own involvement and pinning the blame on each other, they had, in fact, operated as a single unit, a pack with a pack mentality. All of them said each of the others had sex with the victim and all agreed that Anita had to die. Although Travers was the catalyst and the one who did the killing, the others were complicit in the act and there is no evidence that any of them tried to stop him. In the heat of the night, they were each consumed by the group's lust.

It is extraordinary that a teenager such as Travers could influence gaol-savvy criminals such as the Murphys, especially 33-year-old Mick Murphy, a gaol escapee. 'In my opinion, Travers ran the show,' says Detective Paul Rynne. 'If Travers said "jump", the others would say "how high?"' It was worse than that. When Travers indulged in acts of bestiality and rape, the others laughed and encouraged him.

While there are general similarities in the families in which Travers, Murdoch and the Murphy brothers belonged – large, single-parent families, poorly educated with a low standard of living – the group also shared certain psychological traits common among groups of criminals.

Travers was a true psychopath. He had no emotional attachment to anyone and was completely ego-centric. Everyone else in his social and familial circles were objects to be manipulated and exploited for his own gratification. His friend Michael Murdoch had feelings and emotions, but because of a lack of familial attachments, he formed a relationship with Travers that was entirely toxic, frequently criminal and ultimately murderous.

The amazing thing about all five men was that at the time of the rape and murder, they all had girlfriends and were in fairly stable relationships. Les Murphy, who already had two children to another partner, was living with 17-year-old Lisa Travers and her daughter in the caravan behind Travers' home. Travers' girlfriend, 'a 15-year-old girl with short brown hair, pimples and braces' named Karen, was going to escape with him to New Zealand and continued to visit him throughout the trial. Gary Murphy had 'women coming out his ears', according to one report. With two children to an earlier girlfriend, he had been living with another woman for four years before the murder. Mick Murphy also had a new girlfriend when he was arrested. Scratched into the wood of the prisoner's dock in Central Court were the words 'Mick L Leanne 1987'.

So sex, or a lack of it, was not the issue. In the 12 months before the Cobby murder, the men's attacks on women escalated to a point where murder was an almost inevitable outcome of the group's criminal behaviour. Anita Cobby's killers confirmed 'every assumption we have about those who commit violent crime … poor, from broken homes with little to no prospects for the future.'

The events in Reen Road, Blacktown, in February 1986, however, most likely had their genesis in the 'dismal childhoods' of the men responsible. 'If these families were given proper support, their sons would not turn into car thieves, armed robbers, sexual deviants and murderers,' maintains Ian Kennedy, who continues to work in the NSW justice system, although he is no longer a serving detective. His former colleague Garry Heskett is not as forgiving. 'Given it was a classic needless crime, it's hard to have too much empathy for the men involved.'

American psychologist Samuel Yochelson began studying criminal behaviour in the early 1960s in a Washington DC hospital. By the end of the decade, when he was joined by Stanton Samenow, they began one of the longest studies conducted of criminal offenders. Their study of causality in criminal behaviour was expected to identify 'internal conflicts and childhood fixations' as the root cause of criminality in individuals. The attempted manipulation of results by their subjects, however, led the psychologists to look at cognitive failures in criminals from a wide range of socioeconomic and ethnic backgrounds.

Basically, they found that criminality was a result of 'cognitive distortions' formed in early childhood years. Children learn at an early age to exploit people in their own families to achieve their goals, which are often self-centred and power-orientated, and when adults lack the ability to maintain control they reinforce these improper patterns of thinking that are still developing. Eventually, without correction and direction, these children start to emulate the behaviour of older models who they perceive are in control and have power.

Among the more than 50 different errors in thinking and judgement displayed by criminal subjects in their ground-breaking study, Yochelson and Samenow were able to determine the following broad generalisations of negative behaviours among criminal inmates:

Criminals are fearful … of failure, of being viewed as weak and of being perceived as not in control. They compensate for their insecurity by seeking power and control, and by interacting with others in a secretive and manipulative manner.

Criminals remove all internal and external deterrents … they justify their actions, blame others, make excuses and lie so there are no compelling reasons to avoid such behaviours.

Criminals are predators who pursue power and control … through intimidation, humiliation and abuse of power.

Criminals demand to be seen as unique … they compensate for a lack of self-confidence by speaking about themselves in grandiose terms.

Criminals feel victimised and angry when they don't get their own way … they play the part of the victim in order to manipulate the sympathies of others. Instead of expressing self-blame, they react with anger and vengeance towards those they blame for their circumstances.

Criminals fail to think long term … they avoid consideration of potential negative consequences and regularly act on impulses within an unsubstantiated mindset.

The major criticism of Yochelson and Samenow's study over the decades is that they tended to discount environmental and internal psychological factors that have since been found to contribute to criminality. They also pay little attention to the cultural factors that impact on a person's cognitive development and the presence of 'survival mechanisms' often employed by economic and racial minority groups. It is clear that many criminal behaviours are often condoned by the particular subculture to which the individual belongs, so it is not enough to blame 'cognitive distortions' as the ultimate cause of all individual criminality.

Psychologist Hans Eyseneck states that higher levels of testosterone are associated with a higher degree of psychoticism. For this reason, extreme displays of aggression, hostility and anger, as well as a tendency to be highly manipulative and unsympathetic, are typically present in male criminals. He could have been talking about John Travers or any of the Murphy brothers.

Eyseneck says the more neurotic and extroverted a criminal, the less conditionable they are … thus we often have an individual like Travers, or even Mick Murphy, who is predisposed to react impulsively to external stimuli with anger and aggression and cannot prevent those impulses from being externalised even when the threat of consequences is clearly present. Similarly, the neurotic introvert is more inclined to react with 'desperation, despondency and paranoia'.

Both types of offender have major defects in displaying empathy, are susceptible to criminality and are equally dangerous. Given that the five men involved in the Cobby case also shared a violently misogynist mindset that reduced women to sex-objects, it was a psychological powder keg.

Thus we have Travers and Mick Murphy, two neurotic extroverts, leading a band of introverts – Murdoch, and Les and Gary Murphy. Travers, particularly, is the classic 'ego-directed offender', one who 'engages in deviance because of a deficient self-concept.' For Travers, criminality, or least the consequent lifestyle, was a source of self-esteem. The primary objective of the ego-directed offender is to lessen the impact of a deficient self-image. They typically do this by seeking power and control.

Another characteristic of the men's behaviour was a perceived lack of empathy and sympathy for their victims. At the time of the trial, and in the many years later, the five men never publicly expressed their sorrow for what happened to Anita Cobby … not because they forgot to but because they didn't feel any. They only felt regret for their own situation.

In developmental terms, empathy develops as egocentricity recedes, such as when a child learns to view the world from someone else's perspective. Whereas empathy is seen as a cognitive awareness of another person's emotional state, sympathy is an automatic personal emotional response to a situation. Sympathy precedes empathetic awareness, but empathy towards someone, even the victim of a crime, does not automatically elicit sympathy … especially in a criminal mind.

Lawyer Leigh Johnson maintained that John Travers was 'deeply' and 'genuinely' sorry for what he had done but was high on drugs at the time of the murder. Travers allegedly told Johnson, 'I know I did it. I had no idea what I was even doing. Totally off my head.' Travers was also allegedly remorseful that 'he got others into it.' Even if his sentiments are true, they're a long way short of an apology.

In 1989, Travers' mother died at the age of 39. He was escorted from gaol in handcuffs, wearing a new suit and sunglasses to attend his mother's funeral, after being released on 'compassionate grounds'. The service was at Pinegrove Memorial Park in Western Sydney, not far from where Anita

Cobby's ashes are interred. In the 30 years he has been in gaol, Travers has been able to maintain some family relationships. He has been visited by his sister Lisa, some of his brothers and various nieces and nephews over the years. But there is little evidence that he is remorseful or has sought to rehabilitate himself in gaol.

On 6 June 1996, Travers was being transported from Goulburn Gaol's maximum security to Long Bay Gaol with two other prisoners when he was seen by guards 'acting suspiciously' in the van on closed circuit TV. The van made a detour to Bowral Police Station and all three were charged with attempting to hacksaw their way out of the van.

After his escape attempt in 1996, Travers was categorised as an extreme high-risk inmate, which was downgraded to high security in 1997, and moderate high security in 1998, before this was revoked by the Police Commissioner in 2001. In Goulburn Supermax, Travers is the subject of a system alert that prevents him from associating with certain other inmates, including Bronson Blessington, one of the Janine Balding murderers.

Due to the nature of his crime, Travers has been fearful for his own safety in gaol. He has been to Long Bay Hospital on several occasions, and has been segregated for several months at a time for threatening the safety of a correctional officer, for fighting and for having unauthorised property in protective custody. He remains in segregation block Unit 7 with other high profile 'lifers', such as backpacker killer Ivan Milat.

Michael Murdoch, the youngest of the killers, has been bounced around a number of gaols starting with Parklea, then Goulburn, Windsor, Lithgow, Bathurst and Junee. He went from an A2 Maximum Security to B classification (medium) before the less severe classification was revoked when another prisoner said he allegedly feared for his life from Murdoch in 2002. He was segregated for a short time, which affected his good order and discipline ranking within gaol, when he was allegedly linked to a mobile phone that was found in a protected area.

After an altercation with one of the Murphy brothers, Murdoch was deemed not suitable for transfer to Goulburn because he has 'problems' with John Travers. He has been visited by his brother, cousins and several friends, and has become a committed Christian. Relatively well-behaved, some years ago he was allegedly provided with some legal help to try and get a parole date hearing, but 'didn't get to first base'.

Les Murphy, the youngest of the Murphy brothers, is the only one of the five men convicted with the possibility of parole. When he was sentenced to life imprisonment, he was given a non-parole period of 34 years, but it is unlikely he will ever be released. Murphy has a long list of associates in Goulburn Gaol with whom he is not allowed to mix and has been in trouble for failing a urine test, failing to provide a urine test and fighting. During lawyer John Marsden's defamation action against Channel 7 in 2001, it was alleged that Les Murphy had threatened a fellow prisoner who was going to testify against Marsden, causing the witness to withdraw.

Opened in 2001, the Super Maximum facility is located within the grounds of the Goulburn Correctional Centre. Initially called the High-Risk Management Unit (HRMU, which inmates quickly renamed 'HARM-U'), it was Australia's first Supermax gaol since the closure of the Katingal facility at the Long Bay Correctional Centre in the late 1970s. The facility is the most secure gaol within the NSW gaol system.

A 2008 report by the New South Wales Ombudsman stated that there is 'no doubt … that the HRMU does not provide a therapeutic environment for these inmates.'

That description might just satisfy enough people that 'natural lifers' such as the Cobby killers are doing their time just a little bit tougher. John Travers has marked every significant birthday since his arrest in high security gaols – he turned 21 at Maitland Correctional Centre; 30 at Goulburn Correctional Centre, 40 at Lithgow Correctional Centre and will more than likely spend his 50th birthday, and every birthday to come, in Goulburn's Supermax.

CHAPTER EIGHTEEN

The Legacy

'Anniversaries? I never forget what happened, when and where it happened, but it is part of history and it's been time to move on for a long time. I went to the funerals of Garry and Grace Lynch out of respect for them. Without their assistance and their cooperation with the press that allowed details about their daughter to get out there and shock the public so they would come forward, the case may not have been solved. I truly believe that.

Former detective, Ian Kennedy

Garry and Grace Lynch were going through the horror of attending the murder trials of the five men accused of murdering their daughter when they reached out to another family reeling from the after effects of a murder. In June 1987, five-year-old Tess DeBrincat was shot and killed while she was setting the family table for dinner in her Quaker's Hill home. A neighbourhood dispute led two drug addicts to fire on a house in Hillcrest Road, the wrong house was targeted and an innocent life was lost.

The following year, the Lynches were asked to meet the Balding family, whose 20-year-old daughter Janine had been kidnapped from Sutherland Railway Station in her own car by a group of street kids. The culprits had driven west and raped Janine, then dumped her body in a dam in Minchinbury, only a kilometre or two from where Anita Cobby's body was found. The case against those responsible – 22-year-old Stephen 'Shorty' Jamieson, 16-year-old Matthew Elliott and 14-year-old Bronson Blessington – was strengthened by use of DNA technology for the first time in solving a murder.

The murder of Janine Balding, with its echoes of the Anita Cobby, shocked hardened detectives and the wider community. Janine was buried in her hometown of Wagga Wagga while her family and friends were left to grieve for a life lost so young, so pointlessly. The Lynches later spent some time with Bev and Kerry Balding in Cronulla, and again at the Baldings' home in Wagga. The Baldings were heartened by the community support they received, especially from the Lynch family, but nothing prepared them for the trial and subsequent political fallout that put a cloud over the case for the next 20 years.

'Up until talking with the DeBrincats and Baldings,' Garry Lynch recalled, 'we'd had no chance to really share those bleak years after Anita's murder.' Garry and Grace Lynch brought comfort to these families – who were struggling to come to terms with the loss of their loved ones to homicide – because the Lynches had lost so much themselves.

In 1990, Garry Lynch was invited by Michael Yabsley, the NSW Minister for Corrective Services, to join the board of the Serious Offenders Review Board. It was the first time a victim of crime had been asked to monitor and assess serious offenders and make recommendations regarding their lives in gaol and their possible release. 'I felt greatly honoured that I had been asked, and a little terrified because I'd never been in gaol before and I would be coming face to face with some of our worst murderers. It was very daunting.'

The NSW Government received complaints from academic bodies and church groups to sack Lynch before the first meeting because they were afraid that he would take out his 'animosity and revenge' for his daughter's murder on the gaol system. Nothing could have been further from the truth.

The first meeting of the Serious Offenders Review Board (SORB, later Council) replacing the old Release on License Board, occurred in February 1990. The new board consisted of ten men headed by Judge KF Torrington.

Each prisoner in NSW has a classification, with those sentenced to life classified A1. If there is a period of good behaviour in gaol, they may then be reclassified A2. Then there are other B and C level classifications, which also determine which gaol offenders are sent to.

When Lynch joined the board, there were more than 350 'life' prisoners in NSW gaols, and there had been continued community anger over the release of violent prisoners.

In his work with the Serious Offenders Review Board (later Council) from 1990 to 1995, Garry Lynch visited gaols and talked with some of Australia's most notorious criminals. In between regularly monthly meetings, members of the board would visit NSW gaols and talk with gaol governors, staff and various 'life' prisoners. In gauging the progress of prisoners during their custodial sentence, it was felt the board was better equipped to make recommendations on prisoners' reclassifications and possible release. Lynch did this job not out of any self-interest but, even more remarkably, to 'facilitate their progress through the gaol system'.

Garry was visiting a High Security wing at Goulburn Gaol, before the Supermax opened, when he was shown a three-man cell, with three bunks and a shower.

'There were two giants standing in the cell but I sensed another presence, a much smaller man, over in a corner on my right. I had a quick look at him and I thought he had a wart on his left cheek, but then I realised it was a not a wart, it was a little tattooed teardrop – Travers' trademark. I was looking at Travers. He just flicked his eyes at me, and the superintendent said to him, "What do you think of the cell?" "I don't know. It's the only one I've been in."'

Garry backed out quickly because he realised the potential for generating embarrassing headlines such as 'Anita Cobby's father confronts her killer.' He was later informed that Travers had complained about Garry going into his cell because it was 'a bad omen.' Although it clearly rattled him at the time, to Lynch, Travers was already dead ... 'a negative creature'. 'He meant nothing to me ... he no longer had any connection with my daughter.'

Garry Lynch always thought that if he met one of his daughters' killers he would 'rip their throats out' but he no longer had the hate or anger in him to do it. 'I'd forgiven his soul, not his actions, and this is good to my mind.'

Whenever one of the five were interviewed by the Board, Garry Lynch would excuse himself from the meeting. On one occasion, however, there was no order to the prisoners coming into the room and before they realised, Les Murphy was standing at the door. Garry quickly rose to his feet and excused himself.

'Mr Lynch, I'd prefer if you stayed,' Les Murphy interjected. Garry looked at Judge Gee and said, 'No. I think it would be better if I withdrew.'

Later that day a prisoner came in with a letter from Les Murphy for Garry Lynch. It read:

Dear Mr Lynch,
I am sorry that I never said much. I really want to talk to you. I guess I'll just have to wait until next time. What I want to say is that I am sorry for what happened. I hope you will forgive me. Thank you.
L Murphy

Lynch observed the 'tough little man' with the 'swaggering gait'… the man who had allegedly kicked his daughter when she was begging for her life. The Gaol Governor told Lynch that Murphy was a 'hoon' who 'hung out with the heavies'. Sometime later, he received another letter from Murphy via his solicitor, asking for forgiveness. 'I wrote and thanked the solicitor and left it at that.'

Lynch met the four men who were gaoled for the murder of Janine Balding in 1988, including the youngest, Bronson Blessington, and John Glover, the infamous 'Granny Killer'. In his five years on the Council, he met 'many remorseless killers who had nothing but complaints on how hard their life was in gaol … [but] not a thought for their victims or their families.'

Garry Lynch was personally criticised and bailed up in the street by private citizens who thought he was responsible for releasing dangerous prisoners back into the community. He patiently explained that the Serious Offenders Review Council makes recommendations to the Commissioner of Corrective Services, which in turn makes recommendations to the NSW Supreme Court, which then refers the case to the Offender Review Board. The Commissioner of Corrective Services makes the ultimate decision regarding the release of a prisoner.

In November 1992 John Merrick, the chief grief counsellor from Glebe Coroner's Court, approached the Lynches about meeting the Simpson family. The previous August, the Simpson's nine-year-old daughter Ebony had been abducted, raped and murdered coming home from school in the township of Bargo, south of Sydney. The circumstances of this particular crime were as chilling as the Cobby case, and the Simpson family were understandably struggling to come to terms with the tragedy.

A man named Andrew Peter Garforth had snatched Ebony from the bus stop at about 4pm and put her in the boot of his car. Seven kilometres away, the 31-year-old raped the little girl, tied her hands and feet and threw her into the dam. As Garforth walked away, Ebony Simpson was crying out for help as she drowned. He then went home to his own wife and two children as if nothing had happened. The following day, he changed the appearance of his car a little by removing the grill and joined the search party for the missing girl, even parking his car out the front of the Simpson house where the search party was being coordinated.

That was his undoing.

An eyewitness had seen a brown car in the vicinity of the bus stop the previous day, and a general description of a white male with long stringy hair was circulated. Mr Peter Simpson remembered the man and the car from nine days previously when he picked up Ebony from the bus stop. The stranger had the car bonnet up and Mr Simpson actually asked him if he needed help. The car and description of this man matched the suspect, and police were later amazed to find the car parked out the front of the Simpson home. When Garforth returned to the car, he was spoken to by detectives and taken in for questioning. During a second interview, he admitted that he had thrown the little girl into the dam.

'I got a phone call from John Merrick, the NSW Coroner's welfare counsellor who informed me Mr Simpson wasn't dealing well with the death of his daughter Ebony,' says Ian Kennedy. 'He knew I had great success with Garry Lynch and he was wondering if Garry could talk to the Simpsons. I was certainly happy to ask him and Garry said yes straight away.

'He met the Simpsons and helped them in the grieving process … the counsellors realised that getting people who had been through this grief was the best way to help others in the same situation, and that was the start of the Homicide Victims Support Group.'

The sad reality was, in the more than six years since the Anita Cobby murder, there was still no formal counselling process or support mechanism for families and friends dealing with the trauma of murder. 'There was no counselling,' Grace Lynch remarked years later. 'There wasn't any support really, except from our friends … I think the victims of crime, the surviving victims, felt that we'd been able to go on with our lives and somehow it gave them strength to go on with their lives too.'

Garry Lynch accompanied the Simpsons to Bowral Court where Andrew Garforth stood trial in 1993. Some people contacted radio stations and complained that Garry was trying to garner 'publicity for himself' by attending the court. 'I remember thinking how ridiculous that was,' says Peter Simpson, 'as if he hadn't had enough publicity in his life … he's just trying to lighten someone else's burden, and I for one am very grateful for that.'

The Simpsons despaired there was not 'more consideration in the way the judicial system treated victims left behind after murder.' It took seven judges to put Andrew Garforth away for the rest of his life. After the first trial, in which the killer was gaoled for life without parole, he went through two appeals before three-judge benches. Garfield twice appealed his life sentence because he felt the crime was not in the 'worst possible case' scenario and put the Simpson family through another 'two and a half years of pure hell'.

In August 1993, John Merrick suggested the Lynches, the Simpsons and Maya Hessels, the mother of 16-year-old Nigel Hessels who was murdered in 1992, form a support group for family and friends of murder victims. The Homicide Victims Support Group first met on 7 September 1993 at the Institute of Forensic Medicine at Glebe with Martha Jabour the coordinator.

Nine families were initially involved in the HVSG. The aim of the group focused on support, education and reform. 'Some victims bring with them a lot of anger, hurt and feelings of revenge,' said Garry. 'The saddest thing is that at each meeting there are new victims … '

'I went to the first couple of meetings and, later on, I became the boss of Homicide for the Southern region,' says Kennedy. 'People would stand up, say their name and who their loved one was who was murdered. The Lynches encouraged others … the bravery people were showing was enormous and they often got a round of applause at the end of their talk. They've had great success over the years because it's a great form of therapy for people.

'It's a shame that something like that wasn't available in the 1950s and 1960s. It would have saved a lot of pain and suffering … We learned a lot from [Anita Cobby's] case and we passed it on. Garry and I went down to the Police Academy at Goulburn and lectured what to do at a crime scene.'

The Lynches had nothing but praise for the police who worked on Anita's case, but meeting many other people through their support group they realised that, for whatever reason, some families dealing with the aftermath of murder did not get the same level of support. 'Despite the fact that many of us were still hurting,' Garry said, 'we spoke in a rational, clearheaded manner, without malice, just telling our story and talking about things we felt the police could have done better.'

The group received a standing ovation from the group of 60 police cadets. '[It was] the greatest thing that we've ever heard,' says Ian Kennedy, 'because we'd been under a delusion how we should approach a family after a homicide. We know better now.'

The HVSG even became part of the syllabus at Goulburn Police Academy.

The HVSG also articulated the need for a retreat for family members of murder victims and, after two years of hard work, Ebony House was opened in 1995 at Garrawarra Hospital, near Helensburgh, south of Sydney. The house was named in honour of Ebony Simpson and is used by people who are dealing with grief or attending court cases.

'The idea is that people can go there when they're left behind after a murder and stay or visit, and be with other people for an afternoon or a weekend, and see that people can get on with life and be positive … ' explained Garry Lynch.

Since then, the HVSG have initiated and advised on many changes to the criminal justice system in a constructive and dignified manner. They have also been consulted regarding the framing of laws involving all the victims of crime, not just homicide victims. Some of the legislated changes have involved issues dealing with compensation, victims' rights, court delays, home invasion laws, knife laws, police powers and diminished responsibility. Other changes include changes to 'bail and parole, weekend detention, early release programs, the determination of life sentences, victim impact statements, victims registries, jury preparations, direction of the defence case, the naming of juveniles, standard minimum sentences, related health issues, forensic procedures and many more'.

The HVSG are now government funded because of their success and have given victims of homicide a voice, which previously they didn't have, and other countries have followed their lead. Although Garry Lynch resigned from the Serious Offenders Review Council in 1995 because he 'couldn't look victims of crime in the eye' once he was working with HVSG, he appreciated that some good had come out of the horror his family went through.

'If I didn't do that for others,' he once said, 'it would destroy me … '

Epilogue

Is it possible to quantify murder? Was the Anita Cobby case the worst ever? How do you compare a crime that is so shocking in its own right to the murder of Janine Balding in 1988? The offenders in that case were even younger than the Cobby killers. What about the murder of Ebony Simpson, who was only nine years old when she was abducted, raped and drowned in a dam?

The simple answer is you can't. Every murder is a tragedy … someone's life has been taken and often there is a complete randomness to the crime.

The abduction, rape and murder of Leeton schoolteacher Stephanie Scott is a heartbreaking echo of the Cobby murder – she was allegedly taken by a 'reclusive loner' while working at her school on Easter Saturday in order to leave work for her students while she was to be away on her honeymoon.

It's as if every generation has one particular crime that defines it for all time. The Anita Cobby case was that crime for many people.

'Those crimes that have a component relating to sexual assault and sexual deviancy have both a devastating effect on those close to the victim and a corrosive effect on those close to the perpetrators,' says Garry Heskett. 'It was just not the victim who was affected, it was their family, their relatives, their close friends, the neighbourhood and socially, the entire community. It affects everyone …'

The Homicide Squad today do a tremendous job, utilising CCTV footage, digital tracking and forensic DNA technology to solve crimes, which have each made a huge difference to policing. It's interesting to imagine the impact any of these innovations – let alone the use of digital recording during police interviews, which is standard practice today – would have had on the Cobby investigation. The case may have been over in three days rather than three weeks.

In the end, however, there are no real winners, and no complete closure for the families of victims of crime, except for the satisfaction that the police were able to bring the five men responsible to trial and successfully sought their conviction. In many ways, however, the Anita Cobby case was atypical in that it resulted in a successful investigation, prosecution and conviction, with harsh sentences handed down to those who were found guilty that were not successfully appealed. That the law of the land was actually changed to keep the guilty in gaol for the rest of their natural lives makes this case even more extraordinary.

'I do think the system is pretty good now and should ensure these blokes die in gaol,' says former *The Sun* editor John Benaud. 'Non-parole periods for major crimes do seem to be more in line with community thinking.'

And it will be a hard, long sentence for the men. The human reality of 'life in gaol without parole' was highlighted in a 1995 United Nations paper on life imprisonment:

'Social isolation, total dependencies, supervision of time, prolonged sexual abstinence, loneliness and loss of responsibility, combined with a regimentation and routine isolation of life … [it is an] extreme form of life punishment in the real sense of the word.'

But the five killers are not the only ones doing hard time. The families of Travers, Murdoch and the Murphys have also had their share of public shaming and vilification.

The mothers of both Travers and Murdoch died prematurely – in the same year, within four months of each other, in 1989 – and their families believe a 'broken heart' was just as much a factor in their deaths as their ongoing health issues. The three families of the murderers have tried to fade into the background in the ensuing decades. The majority of the large Murphy clan had a falling out with their imprisoned siblings, while familial support for Travers and Murdoch has been sporadic over the years.

In 2001, Lisa Travers wrote a letter to the *Blacktown Sun* that gave the public a rare insight into how the families of the killers were treated:

'The threats started coming; people wanting to kill us,' she wrote, '[to] do the same to me when we were just as innocent as Anita. But because we carry the Travers name, somehow that makes us all guilty, makes us bow our heads in shame. It's us – the Travers on the outside – that are continually being tortured for a crime the rest of us didn't commit…

Do you really think all this publicity affects the guilty? They are in gaol and are never getting out. They got what was the maximum penalty the law could provide. They are locked away from society and have no clue as to what's going on. I don't want sympathy. I just want our children to have opportunities, not discrimination.'

The letter was only published after consultation with Grace and Garry Lynch. Even the Lynches, in their old age, could empathise with other people who were indirectly affected by their daughter's death. Garry suffered from Alzheimer's disease in his final years, passing away at the grand age of 90 in 2008. Grace followed five years later after a short battle with cancer. Their ashes rest in the same garden as their daughter Anita at Pinegrove Memorial Park in Minchinbury.

'One of the things Garry Lynch asked me before he died was, "Please, don't let Anita's memory fade,"' remembers Garry Raymond, who was one of the driving forces behind a planned annual memorial to Anita Cobby. The event was organised by the Retired Police Association, of which Garry is chaplain, at Pinegrove on the 29th anniversary of her death. The first public memorial to Anita, the service was planned as a 'celebration of Anita's life and a way to spread the message of zero tolerance towards violence against women.'

In a nice touch, instead of flowers, it was promoted that donations could be made to the '20th Man Fund' which helps disadvantaged youth. 'If we can get these men when they're young and turn their attitudes around to respecting women, to getting some sort of career or job going, to get some self-esteem, then they won't perpetrate these crimes," Garry Raymond said. 'We want to reach out to the younger generation and show them the lessons that we've learnt."

The first memorial drew Anita's younger sister Kathryn back into the media spotlight, a position she has shunned for the last three decades. Having remarried and now the mother teenaged twins, Kathryn and her family also fund the Anita Cobby Nursing Scholarship to support the careers of young nurses. In 2014, a local park in Sullivan Street, Blacktown, where the Lynch family lived, was dedicated in her honour and renamed 'Anita Cobby Reserve.'

'I do feel close to her still to this day,' Kathryn said at the time. 'It's a nice feeling to think she's still there looking down and protecting me and my family."

But the planned memorial to mark the 30th anniversary may be the family's last involvement in a public ceremony for some time. In an email to the author, Kathryn said that her involvement in the first memorial took its toll on her and she did not like to bring attention to herself and her young family. It was time for everyone to move on, but not to forget.

Anita Cobby cannot speak for herself, and so her story will always be incomplete. That's the real tragedy of the case, 30 years later.

Perhaps the epitaph on her grave, specially chosen by her family, covers all that is still left unsaid.

'Her light shines forever.'

Timeline of Events

2 November 1959: Anita Lorraine Lynch born in Sydney, NSW.

27 March 1982: Anita Lynch marries fellow nurse John Cobby.

2 February 1986: Having returned home to live with her parents in Blacktown, Anita Cobby is abducted, raped and murdered on her way home from work.

3 February 1986: Garry Lynch reports his daughter missing.

4 February 1986: The body of a young woman is found in a paddock in Prospect by farmer John Reen. Later that day, the body is formally identified as belonging to Anita Cobby. An autopsy is then performed by Dr Joe Malouf.

6 February 1986: The NSW State Government posts a $50,000 reward for information leading to the capture of Anita Cobby's killers.

9 February 1986: Re-enactment of Anita's last movements using Constable Debbie Wallace.

10 February 1986: The body of Anita Cobby is cremated after a funeral service at Pinegrove Memorial Park.

21 February 1986: The NSW State Government doubles the reward for information to $100,000.

23 February 1986: Miss X tapes her conversation with John Travers.

24 February 1986: Michael Murdoch and Les Murphy re-arrested. Travers, Murdoch and Les Murphy implicate each other, as well as Mick and Gary Murphy, in the crime.

26 February 1986: Mick and Gary Murphy arrested at a townhouse in Glenfield. Later that day, they make their first appearance at Blacktown Court before joining Travers, Murdoch and Les Murphy at Westmead Coroner's Court.

23 June 1986: Travers, Murdoch and the three Murphy brothers appear for their committal hearing at Glebe Coroner's Court.

1 July 1986: The five men are committed to trial by Magistrate Derrick Hand.

16 March 1987: John Travers pleads guilty. The trial of Michael Murdoch and the three Murphy brothers begins at Darlinghurst Criminal Court, Sydney.

17 March 1987: First jury dismissed after trial is aborted.

23 March 1987: Second trial begins.

15 May 1987: The jury is taken to Reen Road, Prospect, to view the crime scene.

10 June 1987: Jury returns a verdict of guilty for all four remaining defendants.

16 June 1987: John Travers, Michael Murdoch and Les, Gary and Michael Murphy are sentenced to life in gaol without parole by Justice Maxwell.

25 June 1987:	Raymond John Paterson is found guilty of being an accessory to murder after the fact after harbouring Gary and Michael Murphy.
3 July 1987:	Two women who allegedly harboured Gary and Michael Murphy stand trial. Mavis Saunders, 19, is given a $1000 good behaviour bond and 24-year-old Debra McAskill is found not guilty.
10 November 1987:	John Travers withdraws his appeal.
7 December 1988:	Michael Murdoch and Mick, Gary and Les Murphy are dismissed by the NSW Supreme Court. All except Mick Murphy are granted special leave to appeal to the High Court of Australia.
30 May 1989:	Michael Murdoch and Gary Murphy have their appeals dismissed by the High Court. Les Murphy's sentence is quashed and he is granted a new trial, but he is not released.
21 July 1990:	Les Murphy is found guilty for the second time.
15 February 1990:	Garry Lynch joins the Serious Offenders Review Board.
7 September 1993:	Homicide Victims Support Group meets for the first time.
14 September 2008:	Death of Garry Lynch, aged 90.
1 July 2013:	Death of Grace Lynch, aged 88.
2 February 2015:	The 29th anniversary of Anita's death is marked by a memorial service at Pinegrove Memorial Park.

Bibliography

Books:

Hand, Derrick and Fife-Yeomans, Janet, *The Coroner* (ABC Books, 2004)

Harmening, William M., *The Criminal Triad: Psychosocial Development of the Criminal Personality Type* (Charles C Thomas Publisher, 2014)

Lennox, Gina (editor), *Forged by War: Australians in Combat and Back Home* (Melbourne University Publishing, 2006)

Lennox, Gina as told by Garry Lynch, *Struck by Lightning* (Allen and Unwin, 1996)

Sheppard, Julia, *Someone Else's Daughter: The Life and Death of Anita Cobby* (Ironbark Press, 1991)

Various authors, *Anita and Beyond* (Penrith Regional Gallery & The Lewers Bequest, 2003)

Whiticker, Alan, A*nother Twelve Crimes That Shocked the Nation* (New Holland Publishers, 2008)

Whiticker, Alan, *Twelve Crimes That Shocked the Nation* (New Holland Publishers, 2005)

Articles:

Anderson, Dr John, 'Indefinite, Inhumane, Inequitable' – A Reform Agenda (unsw.edu.au, 2006)

Heskett, Garry, 'Remembering the Anita Cobby Investigation' (*Australian Police Journal*, March 2003).

McNeice, Graham, Garry and Grace Lynch interview transcript (2005).

Murphy v The Queen, High Court of Australia 28; 167 CLR 94 (28, 30 May 1989)

Serisier, Tanya, 'Remembering Anita' (HeinOnline, 2005)

Slee, Amruta, 'How Anita Cobby's death changed lives' (*Good Weekend Magazine*, 1 March 2003)

Author Interviews:

John Benaud, Garry Heskett, Ian Kennedy, Garry Raymond, Graham Rosetta, Tony Martin, Tom Sharp and John Wakeling.

Documentaries:

Crime Investigation Australia: The Anita Cobby Murder (Graham McNeice Producer, 2006)

Crime Stories: The Blacktown Boys (Ron Goetz Producer, 2008)

Crime Investigation Australia: Australian Families of Crime (Graham McNeice Producer, 2011)

Newspapers:

Blacktown Sun: 20 November 2001.

Daily Telegraph: 14 January 2015.

Sydney Morning Herald: 26 February 1986; 29 April 1986; 25–27 June 1986; 1 July 1986; 16 March 1987; 18 March 1987; 31 March 1987; 23 April 1987; 1 May 1987; 6–7 May 1987; 12 May 1987; 14–15 May 1987; 12 June 1987; 16 June 1987; 25 June 1987; 1 July 1987; 3 July 1987; 10 November 1987; 8 November 2002; 4 March 2003; 24 September 2005; 14 September 2008; 9 July 2013.

About the Author

Alan Whiticker was born in Penrith, NSW, in 1958. Pursuing the dual careers as a teacher and freelance writer, he emerged as an accomplished writer of sport, history, biography and true crime. In 1997 he completed a Masters Degree in Education and lectured at the University of Western Sydney in 2008. A former Assistant Principal, he is now a freelance writer.

Alan continues to live in Penrith and married to his wife of 33 years, Karen. Alan is the author of 40 books, including *Wanda: The Untold Story of the Wanda Beach Murders* (2003), *Twelve Crimes That Shocked the Nation* (2005), *Crimes of the Century* (2006), *Derek Percy: Australian Psycho* (2008), *Unsolved Crimes: The Cases That Haunt Australia* (2009), *The Satin Man: Uncovering the Mystery of the Missing Beaumont Children* (2013) and *I Survived Kerobokan* (2014, with Paul Conibeer), all with New Holland Publishers.